MAKING MURALS

MAKING MURALS

Clara Wilkinson & Mary West

A practical handbook for wall painting
and mural art to enhance your home

DAVID & CHARLES

www.davidandcharles.com

CONTENTS

BRING NATURE INSIDE WITH A RESTFUL BOTANICAL MURAL –
THIS ONE COMBINES PAINTERLY AND FLAT GRAPHIC STYLES.

INTRODUCTION

As professional mural artists, we want to share with you some of the techniques and styles we have learned over the years designing and painting projects for Living Wall Murals. This book is designed to be a source book of inspiration and a technical step-by-step guide for anyone wanting to design and paint a mural in their own home.

The word mural comes from the Latin *muras*, which means wall. Mural painting is unique because it is, of course, affected by architecture, scale and is a permanent piece of artwork. From the early Renaissance, masters like Leonardo Da Vinci were painting murals, which were often a reflection of day-to-day life. Throughout the 20th century, artists such as Diego Rivera in Mexico became celebrated for their elaborate scenes of life in South America. Street murals became a widespread means of spreading social or political messages, from the post-war Berlin wall, to Northern Ireland during the Troubles, to the images on the Palestinian/Israeli separation wall, to today's street art and graffiti culture epitomized by artists such as Banksy. Domestic murals follow trends in interior design – for example, the recent popularity of hand-painted Chinese wallpapers has filtered down to more accessible wallpaper styles.

Making murals is not just about beauty – it is about expression, spreading a message and wanting to be seen! This is why we love what we do. The freedom and the scale is exciting and daring. For this book, we have chosen some mural styles we think would work well for everyone. There are plenty more to explore, of course, once you have mastered the techniques in this book.

The book is divided into clear sections. First are the materials you will need to get you started, which includes practical items such as ladders, brushes and rollers. We then move on to technical considerations, such as choosing which paints will work on particular surfaces or various finishes. The next section of the book discusses how colours affect light and mood, sourcing ideas, imagery, and how to create your design, including stylistic considerations such as scale and composition. This is followed by information on practical considerations, such as choosing the location of your mural and a suitable style of project for this location, and then preparing the wall and the space. The final sections cover different methods of scaling up your design, techniques of painting and mark-making, and an overview of the main technical painting styles.

The second half of the book is where you can get going yourselves! This is the 'how to' section and it features three basic mural styles for you to choose from, with ten different projects covered in detail. For each of these you will be guided along in steps – from when you set down your ladder to the final brush stroke on the wall. We hope you will find something here to inspire you – happy painting!

Tools

Having the correct materials to hand before you begin is very important. Some items are vital – for example, an assortment of good quality brushes because using your child's poster-paint brush will not give a good result! And you don't want to get halfway through your mural and find you are missing colours that you forgot were on your mood board. You don't need to spend a great deal of money; you may already have items you can make use of – for example, cups and saucers for stencils, or unfinished tins of paint. Here are our personal recommendations – but they are meant as a starting point. You might find you prefer other brands or can utilize different sizes of brush for the marks you wish to make on your mural-making journey.

BRUSHES AND ROLLERS

Walking into an artists' supply shop can feel like an overwhelming experience. This is especially true when shopping for brushes; there is an endless array of shape, style, material and size of brush on display, not to mention a wide differential in price! With so much choice it's easy to get confused, and we have worked our way through half the selection of paintbrushes in our local art supply shops and spent a small fortune. So that you can avoid all this trial and error we have put together a list of essential brushes you will need. You'll be relieved to know that nowadays we keep things simple and rely on an inexpensive and basic line of brushes that work well on most walls. What is worth spending time on is choosing a good selection of brush styles, sizes and shapes. Our suggestions are not finite – with exploration, you may well find a shape and a style that works best for you.

ROUND BRUSHES

Round shaped brushes are the shape we mostly use when painting a wall. They are available in a variety of sizes and bristle types – hog, sable, pony and more, as well as synthetic versions of each (A). Round brushes are available with both pointed (B) and blunt tips (C), each of which has a different use when it comes to painting. We use Da Vinci Fit Synthetics sizes 4 to 16 (see Suppliers).

Pointed round brushes are especially useful for detail and anything like a pointed leaf tip (see Chinoiserie-style Cherry Tree: Step 8) or very precise triangle or curl. The shape is also excellent for varying your line weights. More pressure means a thicker line, less pressure means a narrow delicate line.

Blunt round brushes are a great tool for filling in colour and holding a good amount of paint. They are excellent for carrying different colours in one go – for example, a second colour dipped onto the tip (see Painterly Botanical Mural: Step 7). They are also superb when used at a side angle in a scribbling motion, creating scratchy, textured marks.

D

E

FLAT BRUSHES

Another versatile brush shape is the flat, which is
a rectangular shaped brush with the hair clamped
flat in the ferrule – the metal casing at the end of
the handle (D). There are two types of flat brush,
long flat brushes and small flat brushes. We use
Da Vinci 374 Flat Brushes sizes 4 to 16, or Da Vinci
Nova Synthetics range.

Long flat brushes are, as the name suggests, a
longer squared brush shape (E). This length is
especially useful for holding more paint and liquid,
so if you are painting longer straight edges you
can sweep your paintbrush along without a break
in the mark. The flexibility of the longer hair (it's
a little bit bendy) also allows for dramatic brushy
strokes full of movement.

Small flat brushes are really useful for little
shapes, for producing dabbing marks or for
general shading and blended filling in. They are
great for tight corners or shapes that require a
more structured one-stroke edge. An excellent
example of where we use a flat is for the edges of
a banana leaf (see Birds and Animals); to create
the broken effect 'tears' along the edge the flat
can be utilized to make one dab mark that has
maximum impact.

Flat brushes of all sizes are particularly good at
producing solid lines in varying thickness when
used on their side, depending on the weight you
apply (see Linear Mural).

FILBERT

One of Mary's favourite types of brush, filberts are somewhere between a flat and a round, with long bristles and a flat tip (F). The key noticeable difference is their rounded edge, allowing you to create a variety of marks with a softer line. Filbert brushes come in a variety of lengths and fibre types, meaning that different varieties of filberts will provide different results. A great basic filbert we like to use is the Da Vinci Nova Synthetic in sizes 10 to 18.

THE BEAUTY OF FILBERT FOR A MURAL IS THAT IF YOU CHANGE THE ANGLE OF HOW YOU HOLD THE BRUSH YOU CAN EASILY CREATE INTERESTING SHAPES OR MARKS. ON ITS SIDE, A FILBERT CAN CREATE FLAT FIELDS OF COLOUR EXCELLENT FOR FILLING IN SHAPES AND HOLDING DIFFERENT COLOURS ON DIFFERENT AREAS OF THE BRUSH. THE PARTICULAR ARRANGEMENT OF THE HAIRS AT THE SHAPED END IS ALSO VERY USEFUL WHEN BLENDING LARGE BRUSHY AREAS OF A LEAF FOR THE 'PAINTERLY' TECHNIQUE.

LINER (ALSO CALLED RIGGER OR SCRIPT)

Liner brushes resemble much finer and thinner versions of round brushes (G) and are Clara's firm favourite to work with. Their long length of hair means they are able to hold a lot more paint without the mark drying out on route. This is vital when you need to paint a skinny, steady line in one go. Liners are ideal paintbrushes for Chinoiserie painting because they produce beautifully accurate and delicate lines for long stems, branches or single width edging and shading marks. They are also great for lettering and for any fine detail in general and don't need to be used in the traditional way. We often use them at the end of a project for our touching up – for example, for highlights of white to create light areas or when some dramatic black or gold details are needed.

DECORATORS' BRUSHES

It is useful to have a few decorator (mottler) brushes in your arsenal (H). You will need these for larger scale murals where the design calls for dramatic shapes that need colour to be blocked in quickly. We tend not to use the flat-edge versions, preferring the angled-edge type, but it's up to you. We use Albany 2cm (0.75in) and 2.5cm (1in) sizes.

ROLLERS

Rollers are an excellent tool for quick and easy coverage of a large section of wall (H). They are ideal to use if you plan to paint the wall with a strong base colour – such as for a dark background mural or if your wall needs a refresh. Always buy the best quality roller you can afford and always check at purchase that the roller is compatible with the paint you are using. For quickly filling in large graphic shapes in your design, slim rollers measuring 10–12cm (4–5in) wide are useful. These result in a smoother finish on large, flat-painted shapes. This is also an excellent technique for underpainting large shapes, for example to prepare your design for the painterly technique. Rollers are inexpensive to buy as part of a set (with a slim rolling tray) from any DIY shop (hardware store). In between usage – for example, if you are leaving it overnight – roll the roller in biodegradable cling film (saran wrap) or tie a biodegradable plastic bag tightly around it to prevent drying out.

WHILST NATURAL BRUSHES ARE LOVELY FOR SOME DETAILED PAINTING, IN PARTICULAR OIL PAINTING, WHEN WORKING IN WATER-BASED EMULSIONS (LATEX PAINT) FOR MURALS WE PREFER SYNTHETIC BRUSHES. THEY OFTEN HAVE A SMOOTH FEEL AND THE EVEN CUT OF MANMADE FIBRES CREATES A MORE UNIFORM AND BOUNCY BRUSH. IN PARTICULAR THEY ARE REALLY GOOD FOR NEAT 'CUTTING IN' – PAINTING STRAIGHT EDGES FOR YOUR PAINTED SHAPES. SYNTHETICS DON'T HOLD QUITE AS MUCH LIQUID WHEN PAINTING SO YOU DO NEED TO DIP YOUR BRUSH MORE OFTEN, BUT WE FEEL THIS IS OUTWEIGHED BY THEIR EASE OF USE. THE OTHER BENEFIT OF THE SYNTHETIC BRUSH IS THAT IT WASHES UP QUICKLY AND EASILY.

IF YOU ARE PAINTING AN ENTIRE WALL IN A BASE COLOUR, YOU CAN USE MASKING (LOW-STICK) TAPE ALONG ALL THE TOP EDGES OF ANY AREAS YOU WANT TO PRESERVE, SUCH AS SKIRTING BOARDS (BASEBOARDS) OR LIGHT SWITCHES. FOR THE EDGE OF THE WALL AND CORNERS IT IS OK TO DO THIS, THOUGH THE TRADITIONAL METHOD FAVOURED BY PROFESSIONAL DECORATORS IS TO CUT IN, WHICH MEANS USING AN ANGLED-EDGE DECORATORS' BRUSH TO DRAW A STRAIGHT EDGE LINE. IT'S IMPORTANT TO PAINT THE FIRST LAYER AND THEN 'CUT IN' OR PAINT NEATLY THE EDGES OF YOUR SHAPES WITH A BRUSH. YOU CAN DO A LAYER AT TIME THIS WAY.

G

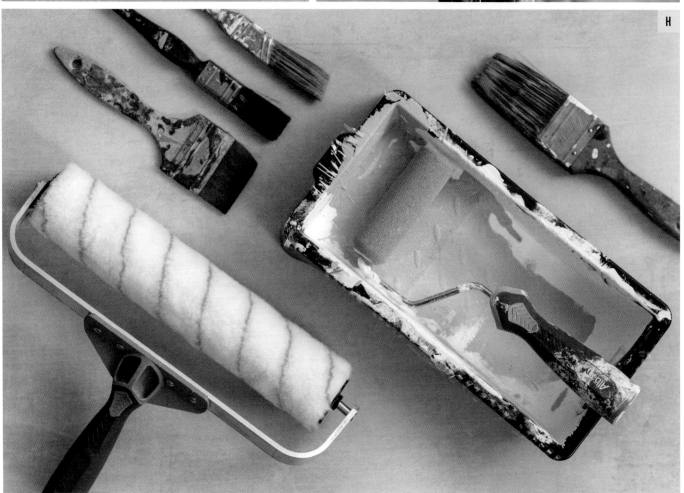

H

OTHER ITEMS

You will also need pencils and sketchbooks for designing, markers for drawing your design onto the wall, stencils for marking out shapes and tape for straight lines and masking.

PENCILS

Drawing pencils come in a range of hardness grades indicated by the numbering on their sides. These are graded in HB scale, with the letter 'H' indicating the hardness of the pencil and the letter 'B' indicating the blackness of the pencil. So the 9H pencil is very hard, whilst the 8B at the other end of the spectrum is very soft and therefore very dark. You may also sometimes see 'F', which indicates a medium pencil that will sharpen to a fine point. For working in a sketchbook we normally use a standard range of pencils that are on the harder spectrum for accuracy – so 2H or F pencils. However, if you want to create a thicker, darker line or shade in your designs, then you can go for 2B to 4B pencils. It's personal preference. When it comes to drawing up your design on the wall a 2B or standard HB works well. This grade is soft enough to be seen clearly, yet easy to rub out if you make a mistake.

SKETCHBOOK AND PAPER

A sketchbook is always more handy than loose paper. You can transport it around and it will store your drawings and designs safely in one place. Go as big as you like, sometimes it's nice to draw out your proposed wall onto a large sheet such as A2. However, we usually work with good quality A3 and A4 sketchbooks such as Daler-Rowney Smooth Cartridge of no less that 130 g/m weight paper. If you use a water-based paint, such as gouache or watercolour, to illustrate your ideas, jot down paint samples or work on a mood board (see Designing a Mural) we recommend choosing a heavyweight specialist watercolour paper no less than 300 g/m weight because this will not buckle or bend when water-based paints are applied. Winsor & Newton sell lovely smooth (hot-pressed) paper pads, which we love to use.

POSCA PENS

Posca pens have transformed the way we draw on a wall – they are paints in a pen form, available in a huge variety of colours and nib sizes. With Posca you are guaranteed a continuous fine line without having to break to re-dip your paintbrush. The paint is chalk and water-based and once on the wall it is hardwearing. Posca pens come in different sizes for varied line thickness and with eight differing nib styles, from the fat PC-17K to the very fine PC-1MC. There is a soft brush tip, an ultra-fine calibrated tip for writing text, and various sizes of bullet tip and flat marker-style chisel tip. We favour the bullet-shaped tip in sizes PC-7M, PC-5M and PC-3M.

STENCILS

Stencils are useful for drawing in shapes accurately if you are less confident freehand. To achieve crisp, accurate, primary shapes we love using any household item such as circular cookie cutters and cups – or Clara has been known to borrow her son's basic shapes stencil kit. For more elaborate shapes that feel daunting, you can use the stencils that are widely available from arts and craft shops. They sell a ubiquitous range of designs, including sturdy flower or leaf shapes. The image won't have much movement, but using a stencil is a good way to practise drawing onto a wall if you feel nervous. You can always rub out and try drawing your own freehand version instead! At the end of this book you will also find some stencil shapes to copy for our most popular designs – a selection of leaves, branches and some fun graphic shapes.

TAPE

A roll of masking (low-stick) tape is a useful part of your kit. We use it to create straight edges for geometric abstract murals (see Abstract Geometric Mural). Different width tape can be fun when used simultaneously, because you can create different sizes of line and shake things up a bit. Tape is also useful to create angular shapes or for areas that you just don't want paint to touch – this includes areas that need protecting, such as skirting boards (baseboards), light switches or electrical sockets. Buy the best quality tape you can find as cheaper versions tend not to stick as well or don't stand up robustly to emulsion (acrylic latex) paint.

Paint

Choosing the right paint for your project is
vital. Paint choice can be divided into two main
categories: for indoor or for outdoor murals.

olive

swedish blue

fleurie

deep adam green

soft green

rose pink

emerald green

yeabridge
green

lamplighter

medic

INDOOR PAINT

Some mural artists like to use acrylics, but we find that they give a plastic finish and offer less breathability. For most indoor projects emulsion (acrylic latex) is the best option – we find that it works much better on the wall, because it is created for this purpose, dries quickly and is hardwearing. Also, depending on your brand choice, it is more eco-friendly.

When choosing paint, first think about where your mural will be. Is it a hardworking hallway, a bathroom that will absorb a lot of moisture, or a child's bedroom that will have to compete with mucky hands? In areas you want to wipe clean, an eggshell (eg-shel) finish works well and will provide a slight sheen. In a bathroom you may choose to go a step further and use a satin finish, although bear in mind it is shinier than an eggshell. We don't recommend the use of gloss paint, which is oil-based, messy and uses thinners such as white spirit (mineral spirits). It is also unforgiving if you make a mistake.

For all indoor projects in this book we have used emulsion. There are many fantastic paints on the market, but – although any brand will do – our favourite is Craig & Rose (A). They have a stunning range of colours in their 1829 Vintage Collection, which offer an exceptional depth of colour as well as excellent coverage that lasts. Their sample pots are often sufficient for most indoor murals – and the sample pots have screw top lids; small things make a big difference!

When needing greater coverage you can match most colours at a local paint shop and have a 1L (1 quart) tin mixed in their own brand. This is more cost-effective than getting large tins of paint from luxury paint suppliers. We have even been known to ask for a colour to match Clara's pink socks (B)!

You may want to explore specialist paint finishes for some designs. For instance, Craig & Rose have products you can apply as a top coat, from Chalk Wash to Glitter Glaze. Look into the options available to you to bring your project to life.

When your mural is finished, you can coat it with a decorators' varnish, which is available in a range of finishes from matt to gloss. This will protect it from finger marks, stains, scuffing and colour fading. We like Polyvine Decorators Varnish.

OUTDOOR PAINT

For most outdoor murals you will need to use exterior masonry paint (C), but if you are working on wood or metal cladding we recommend exterior eggshell (eg-shel). These are both water-based paints, so cleaning brushes is easy. They can be mixed to match colours but do not come in sample sizes, so you need to be sure of the colours you want. We find several layers are needed for good coverage so more paint is required anyway.

Before starting to paint you need to prepare the wall – see Preparation: Preparing Exterior Walls. We use a quick dry stabilizing solution, such as Sandtex Trade Stabilising Solution.

Again, when your mural is finished, you can protect it with decorators' varnish – as for interiors, we like Polyvine Decorators Varnish. Make sure the mural is entirely dry before applying this finishing layer.

CHECK WHETHER YOUR PAINT IS AN
ECO PAINT – ONE THAT HAS LOW VOC
(VOLATILE ORGANIC COMPOUNDS).
THESE NASTY CHEMICALS CAN HAVE
UNPLEASANT SIDE EFFECTS AND ARE
NOT GREAT FOR YOUR HEALTH OR THE
ENVIRONMENT; IF YOUR MURAL IS IN A
CHILD'S ROOM AVOIDING THEM MAY
BE PARTICULARLY IMPORTANT TO YOU.
THERE ARE INDUSTRY STANDARDS FOR
VOC CONTENT IN ALL PAINTS, BUT
WE RECOMMEND USING A LOW VOC
PRODUCT. REALLY GOOD ECO PAINTS
CONTAIN MOSTLY NATURAL INGREDIENTS,
LIKE PLANT-BASED OILS, WAXES, CLAYS
AND CHALKS. THIS COMPOSITION GIVES
BETTER BREATHABILITY, AND NATURALLY
REPELS MOULD. SOME POPULAR ECO
BRANDS ARE FARROW & BALL, LITTLE
GREENE, EARTHBORN, LAKELAND PAINTS,
EDWARD BULMER AND CRAIG & ROSE.
MANY OF THESE BRANDS ALSO USE
SUSTAINABLE PRODUCTION PRACTICES,
SUCH AS RECYCLING FACTORY WASTE
AND ETHICAL SOURCING.

PAINT COLOUR

There are several things to take into account when deciding paint colours. You should think about the space that your mural will inhabit; colour choices have been proven to radically affect mood and emotion, so take into account the amount of time you spend in that room and the atmosphere you want to create. You also need to consider the direction your room faces, because this will have a dramatic effect on colour.

Paint can essentially be divided into warm and cool colours. Warm colours, with red, yellow and orange tones, create warm, lively and inviting spaces. Cool colours, with blue, green and purple tones, generate calm and relaxing spaces, reminiscent of nature. The bedroom should make you feel calm and relaxed and so cool colours are appropriate, whereas dining rooms should make you feel lively and sociable, so are perfect for warm colours. For rooms you don't spend much time in, like a lavatory (powder room), you can really go to town – why not make it an onslaught for the senses!

HOW COLOUR AFFECTS MOOD

Blue

Blue tends to be a calming colour that makes you feel secure and relaxed. It is known to help lower blood pressure and clear the mind. However, paler blues can make a room feel cold (A).

Yellow

Yellow brightens your mood and increases energy. When catching the sunlight it can leave you with feelings of joy and liveliness. A good choice for the kitchen, encouraging a positive start to the day when making that morning cup of tea (B).

Green

Green helps to reduce anxiety. It is one of the most restful colours and is known to be restorative, mind-clearing and to encourage composure. Bring nature inside with a green luscious wall, full of botanical shapes (C).

Red

Red brings drama and energy to a space and can give a very regal feel. However, it is known to raise blood pressure and irritability so it is best kept for rooms that you spend small amounts of time in. Create a rich decadent space in perhaps a downstairs cloakroom (restroom) or a cosy nook (D).

Pink

There is something known as The Pink Effect... exposure to large amounts of pink can have a calming effect and can help relieve feelings of anger and aggression. It has an opposite effect to its primary colour, red. The longer you are exposed to pink, the calmer you will become. Lighter pinks are great for children's rooms and promote feelings of love and playfulness (E).

Black

Be brave with black! It can create an elegant and classic space. Black contrasts beautifully with many other hues and is therefore a perfect backdrop for a mural. Rich accents of colour on top create a warmth and richness to a room and will make a bold maximalist statement (F).

White

White brings a fresh light and airiness to any room and sits well with any colour. Adding a mural to a white space breathes in new life and creates a greater feeling of spaciousness.

HOW LIGHT AFFECTS COLOUR

NORTH-FACING ROOM

Northern light tends to bring out the cooler tones within a colour. It could be a good idea to hang a mirror on the wall to reflect the available light. A north-facing room is the perfect situation for a dark wall – instead of fighting against the gloom, embrace nature and create a cosy, cocooning space (G).

SOUTH-FACING ROOM

These rooms are the most forgiving and can cope with any colour. On sunny days they can be saturated in light from dawn till dusk. If you want to make the most of the feeling of light and space they offer, opt for soft pale tones.

EAST- AND WEST-FACING ROOMS

The light alters throughout the day in these rooms. This can bring quite dramatic changes to your paint choices, but can be rather beautiful to witness. East-facing rooms will flood with light in the morning and become dim in the afternoon. West-facing rooms will be dim in the morning and bathed in light in the afternoon. It might be worth thinking about when you spend time in this room. For instance, if your study is west-facing and you are most productive during the morning, then try using colours that brighten even when the light is dim (H).

ARTIFICIAL LIGHT IS A WHOLE DIFFERENT CAN OF WORMS. HALOGEN AND INCANDESCENT BULBS EMIT YELLOW, WHICH MAKES WALL COLOURS APPEAR WARMER, WHILE WHITE BULBS GIVE OFF A BLUER LIGHT, WHICH MAKES COLOURS APPEAR COOLER.

F

G

H

Designing a Mural

Designing a mural can be one of the most time-consuming parts of the project.
This is the moment to let your imagination run wild and have fun with ideas.
Play with different compositions and colourways and experiment with the actual
application of paint. Once you have fixed upon a theme you can throw yourself
into working out the details.

PREP, RESEARCH AND IDEAS

When designing a mural, inspiration can come from anywhere: magazines; exhibitions; book illustrations; newspaper cuttings; album sleeves; furniture; fashion; nature – we could go on! Depending on the project we take photos, collect printed images and sketch from life. We are always looking!

Think about the atmosphere you want to create in your space. Do you want a calming natural feel (A), or a buzzy, vibrant, knock-your-socks-off look (B)? A strong connection to the natural environment in the home or work place has been proven to enhance emotional wellbeing and alleviate feelings of social anxiety. It also helps people suffering from mental health conditions such as attention and mood disorders. It is for this very reason that many of our murals are botanical; bringing the outside inside.

MAKING A MOOD BOARD

As already mentioned, a most important question to ask yourself is, are you creating a room to spend time relaxing or to feel energized and lively? As outlined in Paint: your colour choices can have a big impact on your mood. If you are computer-confident you could create a digital mood board using a platform like Pinterest. If you are keener on scrapbooking, you can create a physical mood board (C), cutting images from magazines and newspapers, flyers, art postcards, pieces of fabric. Have fun at this stage and try to be as open to ideas as possible.

When working on a botanical mural we sometimes use actual plant cuttings and leaves whilst painting; this will bring an authenticity to your work and make it feel truly alive. Start with line drawings and quick sketches and build up onto

larger sheets of paper (D). When you feel more sure of composition start to experiment with introducing colour (E), perhaps with watercolour or colour pencils initially. If you are confident at using Photoshop or Illustrator this can be a good way to play around with design.

DEVELOPING A PALETTE

When developing a palette you can take inspiration from anywhere. Try looking to the natural world for colour combinations: the yellow of autumn leaves against a bright blue sky; the markings of a tropical fish; a fruit tree bursting with oranges. Look at how artists you admire have used colour – the pop of colours in an Andy Warhol print, or the hues of a David Hockney swimming pool. If fashion is your thing, look at the colour combinations in your favourite fabrics or your most-loved outfit. Think about the furniture in the room chosen for the mural. Do you want to accentuate any of the pieces you own: a pop of pink to match with the pink cushions on a sofa, perhaps, or pastels from a much-loved quilt. The best advice we can give is to go with what you love! This is your mural that you will see every day – it must bring you joy and be a reflection of you and your personality.

CREATING A COLOUR SWATCH SHEET

It is a good idea to prepare with a colour swatch sheet (J). Putting colours next to each other and considering how they work together is an important stage in designing your mural. Don't feel confined to these colours when painting, but this will give you a good overall sense of the palette.

1 Start by gathering a selection of pots of paint in a wide range of colours.

2 Using a sheet of A4 or A3 watercolour paper, paint daubs of the colours you plan to use.

3 Beside each colour jot down the name of the colour and the brand of paint. Seeing the colours lying next each other will enable you to see if they make each other sing.

4 If the mural will have a coloured background, paint this colour over your sample sheet and layer the other colours on top. Colours can look very different depending on the background.

5 We suggest you repeat the whole process two or three times with different palettes each time. You may also want to swap background colours.

USING THE COLOUR WHEEL

Some artists use a colour wheel (M) to choose colours, which will help you understand colour relationships. Complementary colours are those opposite on the wheel, which create the strongest contrast when placed next to each other. For example, red-green, yellow-purple, blue-orange. This can be particularly useful when designing an Abstract Geometric Mural.

CURATED COLOURS

Paint companies sometimes produce curated colour collections. As an example, Farrow & Ball have brought out a Liberty collection (K) and a Natural History Museum collection, creating hand-picked combinations of colour in a cohesive palette. If you feel really stuck, speak to a colour consultant at your favourite company who will be able to offer their advice and expertise.

In order to get a feel for scale and to practise the mural you can try it out on a roll of lining paper (L), which is available from any DIY shop (hardware store). This can then be taped to the wall using masking (low-stick) tape and then painted in situ, using the same emulsion (acrylic latex) you will be using on the wall. Bear in mind that the paint will be absorbed into paper much more easily than into the wall and colours can also look different on paper. Nevertheless this will give you a good feel for how your mural will look.

Depending on the style of mural you want to create, you may want to experiment with the application of paint. For example, when executing a painterly technique the brush marks themselves can become a feature of the design (N). You may wish to incorporate blended areas; this requires practise and an understanding of the consistency of your chosen paint. Chinoiserie-style leaves require a loaded brush and a single sweep, which also requires practise (O).

Painting onto a coloured background can be effective (P). It's also a good way to define a space, framing the mural as it were. You can be playful in extending a design to meander onto ceilings, around doorframes (door casings) or to grow from skirting boards (baseboards). Be as adventurous as you like. When painting onto a dark background underpainting shapes in white can be necessary so lighter colours sing on top (Q).

CHOOSING A SUITABLE MURAL STYLE

So you've decided you'd like to paint a mural – how exciting! But before you get your brushes out and start painting there are a few considerations to bear in mind. Whilst we love spontaneity, it's important first to take a step back and reflect upon the wall you have in mind for your project. Will the delicate floral mural you have your heart set on for the children's play area stand up to lots of little fingers and toy gun wars? Would the neon abstract shapes of a new chimney breast mural get on your nerves after a year?

When choosing where and what to paint it is vital to consider:

- Will your mural be practical in the area of your home you have chosen?

- Will the design work stylistically – can you live with it long term on your chosen wall?

- Have you considered the mural's connection to other influences in the home or garden (yard)? For example, a wall next to doors opening into a garden could depict species of plant in the garden and help to 'bring the outside in'.

PRACTICAL EXAMPLE:
GEOMETRIC HALLWAY

The hallway of Clara's flat (apartment) is large, angular and painted white. The floor is a grey indestructible rubber and against the walls are hooks for bikes and a wooden rack for her three sons to use for their kit. Clara has painted a big mural here that is bright and geometric (A).

It works practically in the space – if knocked about it doesn't matter as its abstract shapes can easily be touched up if necessary (B) and the space lends itself to something bold. This mural also works stylistically because the bold design suits a functional, fun hallway. The style might be less successful in a bedroom, where the desired atmosphere is calm and sleepy. Likewise, a delicate floral design in the hallway would soon get damaged, begin to look shabby and the detail would be overlooked.

STYLISTIC EXAMPLE: LOO WITH A VIEW

'A loo with a view' was our name for a fabulous mural we painted inside a guest cloakroom (restroom). The space was small so we felt confident about painting intricate Chinoiserie on a dark burgundy background. We covered all the surfaces including the ceiling (C).

The design works in a small space due to various factors: it's small, the space is used temporarily for short periods (and not all day) and it has a captive audience – this most private of rooms provides the perfect chance for visitors to see your skill and colours (D). If the same design was in a bathroom or a kitchen it could be overwhelming, but a small space like this allows for bold gestures.

CONNECTION EXAMPLE: GARDEN MURAL

An example of how connections with other influences can work brilliantly is the garden mural we painted in West London. While the space is a family room with a dining table and large open-plan kitchen, the walls face the garden through glass doors.

The client wanted a design that incorporated olive trees, vine leaves, figs and colourful birds to bring the 'outside inside' (E & F).

A

B

C

D

E

F

CHOOSING YOUR SPACE

In Choosing a Suitable Mural Style we discussed the important factors to consider in relation to your chosen location and what style of mural goes where. In this chapter we go a step further, because deciding to paint a mural comes with a set of unique considerations. Unlike painting on standard surfaces, such as paper or canvas, there are some immediate differences and these factors will affect your perspective, composition and shape, negative space and the scale of your mural.

The main differences between a mural and traditional artwork are:

1   A mural covers a vertical (or other angled) space of wall that is connected to the architecture or landscape of a building or exterior wall.

2   Instead of a frame or the edge of a canvas, a mural has no traditional boundaries. Its 'border' becomes the adjoining architecture/structure.

3   A mural is a permanent piece of art that cannot be moved (although it can be painted over). It seems obvious to say it – but a mural is art on the wall!

4   The surface that is being painted can be less predictable (and sometimes more unforgiving) than a safer surface such as canvas.

ARCHITECTURE AND PERSPECTIVE

The architecture of your home or exterior wall is the starting point in any mural. You might have a wall in mind that is screaming at you to be painted. Or you have an idea and you cannot work out which wall to choose. So begin by looking. If you have chosen a wall, is it in close proximity to other strong features, such as bold artworks, items of furniture or does it have shelves in the middle? Is there an ornate fireplace under the wall? Do you have 3m (10ft) high walls or do you live in an old cottage with low ceilings? Maybe your wall has a window intersecting it? Or perhaps the wall is outside and a large shrub covers half of it. Will the wall be viewed from a distance – for example, at the end of a corridor – or will it be only seen up close, for example when lying in the bath?

Take some time to stand looking at your wall from various perspectives. Take note of its surroundings. Take a photograph from the main positions where the mural will be viewed and print it out. This may bring to light the architecture of your space and suddenly illuminate how cluttered/sparse/huge or influenced the wall is by other factors. Consider a simpler design if it's a 'busy' area of the house. Or consider a wow-factor bold number if it's an area that needs jazzing up.

COMPOSITION

Next up for consideration is your composition on the wall, and we suggest starting with less rather than more – you can always add on later. We'll use Chinoiserie trees as an example. Take a photograph of your wall and perhaps print it out onto A4 paper. Cut out shapes from magazines of Chinoiserie wallpaper, or print photographs of trees and cut them out. You can also sketch in your ideas if you prefer.

Try one image of your wall filled to the brim with trees and branches and leaves (A). Then try doing another image very sparsely laid out (B). Concentrate on the negative spaces – these are the areas of wall that remain unpainted and they form shapes all by themselves. Take a look at how these negative space shapes morph when you move the tree trunk or branches around the wall into different configurations. At this stage, it's not about perfection; it's about gaining a sense of abundance versus scarcity on your wall. What sort of design sings for you? Do you prefer the wall when it is entirely covered? Or do you like the uneven negative space that occurs when you move the entire tree to the left-hand section of wall?

As you will see, the areas of negative space are just as important as the filled areas. Think of these areas as a 'holding room' that links the design together. If you completely cover the wall, will it overwhelm the wall and the room? If you leave spaces, does it allow the design to breathe? But if you are keen on a maximalist effect with full coverage, then go for it. More can sometimes really be more! It's all about trying things and having a go.

SCALE AND COMPOSITION

Next try the same exercise with scale and composition; flowers are a perfect way to practise. Using cut-out images again, or drawing in shapes, lay down large flowers onto your A4 wall image. Move the flowers around the wall. Maybe there is a window in the middle – do the flowers work overlapping the window (C)? Or do they work best placed to the side of the window with the window becoming part of the design (D)?

Then on another mock up, draw or place in small flowers instead. Play around with positioning again. Which one looks best? Sometimes scaling up or down dramatically in opposite scale to your wall works brilliantly. Huge shapes on a small wall can look very glamorous (E) and masses of small shapes on a large wall can be gorgeous, too (F & G).

CONTAINMENT AND COMPETITION

Containment traditionally would be the canvas frame or, if no frame, then the negative space surrounding the picture on the wall. This boundary helps define the image as a piece of art. However, a mural has no such boundaries; it creeps and grows wherever it chooses. It can wrap around pillars and under pictures. It can spring from the ground, or wind down from the ceiling. It can be on the ceiling! By its very nature it is part of the architecture or interior, and therefore affects more dramatically where the eye is drawn to within a room. Having no traditional end or boundary means that, as mural artists, we have to make a range of different and sometimes tricky decisions about how our mural will be placed in respect to a wall. Do we want it to control and dominate the wall? Do we need to be respectful of the architecture or features of the room – cornicing or a beautiful archway, for instance? We don't want to overwhelm the wall, or the room, or the outside space. This might all sound rather complicated, but it really isn't. It's about playing around. Thinking about things from another perspective and trying ideas that might not come naturally to you. If you want to upscale then upscale. If you feel like playing it safe then play it safe. There isn't the magic answer and ultimately it's a matter of personal taste. But you never know, you might end up designing and painting something that is completely different to your original idea and works better in your space than the standard off-the-shelf design that you first had in mind!

TECHNICAL PAINTING STYLES

There are many techniques you could draw on when painting your mural but we have chosen three techniques that most of the mural styles in this book use. The linear style is essentially a line drawing on the wall, flat graphic is where you block out shapes in flat single paint colours, and the painterly style is more realistic, with light and shade creating three-dimensional shapes. You might, of course, find that these techniques overlap – as in the *Romeo and Juliet* (below left) and *Kusaki* (below right) murals shown here.

Flat graphic and painterly techniques combined.

Flat graphic and linear techniques combined.

LINEAR STYLE

This style of mural is essentially line drawing on the wall and it does rely on some degree of technical drawing ability. However, with a little practise, and if you keep your shapes simple, it can give a very effective and contemporary feel.

We have two methods of making a linear drawing – either traditionally using a fine paintbrush and paint, or by using Posca pens.

1   Posca pens have transformed the way we draw on a wall. They are paints in a pen form and have a huge variety of colours and nib sizes. With Posca you are guaranteed a fine line without having to make a break and re-dip your paintbrush. The paint is chalk and water-based and once on the wall it is hardwearing.

2   Alternatively you can use a pointed round brush to create your lines, and can achieve different line weights depending on the pressure you use.

3   A dark base colour works really well as a background with a white or metallic line drawing.

4   Or a white base colour looks very striking with a simple black line.

5   The linear technique can also be very effective over the top of a flat graphic or painterly style background.

6   It's important here to have your design drawn out on paper first, either freehand or using templates. Draw the design onto the wall in stages, the largest shapes first to anchor your design. Then add the detail later on.

Adding areas of colour to a linear design can be very effective.

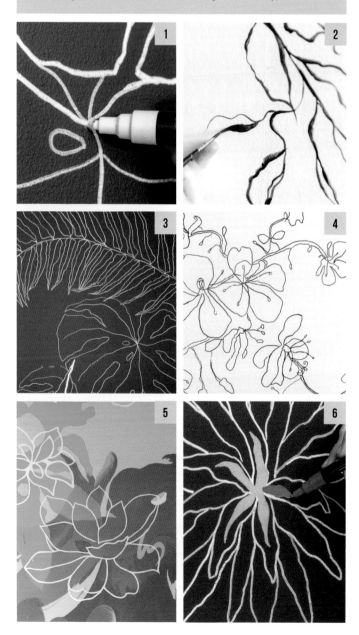

FLAT GRAPHIC STYLE

Flat graphic is essentially a technique where you block out shapes in flat single paint colours – there is little or no tone or variation in shade. If you are new to painting or feeling less confident, we recommend this technique as a good starting point from which to expand your skills. This technique works brilliantly for all styles of design and can become more involved once you gain confidence, for example overlapping the shapes in block colour, or by painting the 'overlap' part of the shape in a different colour.

The key to this style is precision and execution:

1   The style is flat so the paint needs to be uniform. You will perhaps need two or three coats to achieve this, depending on the base wall.

2   Edges need to be precisely executed and gone over with a flat fully loaded brush.

3   For geometric type murals you will need primary shape templates to draw outlines of the shapes. For circles we often use household items such as serving dishes, plates or mugs.

4   Masking (low-stick) tape is used to create straight lines. Peel one end off your tape and stick it down. Gently unwind the tape, smoothing it down as you go. Once you have rolled it out to your desired length, use a credit card to stroke down the length to smooth out any air bubbles. Using another line of the tape, repeat the process adjacent to the first piece of tape. You can choose the width of the gap; 10cm (4in) works well for slim lines or go wider if you'd like.

5   To avoid the paint bleeding underneath the tape, begin painting at one end of the line and work your way down. Always begin each stroke from on the tape, drawing the brush inward onto the wall. If the gap you have allowed on the wall between the tapes is very narrow, then use a slimmer brush to avoid touching the opposite taped edge with your brush.

6   The longer the tape is on, the more entrenched the paint could become – so try not to leave it on overnight if possible. If time is not on your side, then just do sections and move around the wall. Take one end of the tape and slowly and very gently peel it backward, bending it over as you go. Don't lift it outward: lift it ALONG the line of the tape in the direction you are peeling.

Flat graphic in an abstract design.

Flat graphic for botanical shapes.

Flat graphic in a representational design.

PAINTERLY STYLE

This is particularly effective if you want a more realistic three-dimensional looking mural. Although more technically challenging than other techniques, if executed with preparation and care the results can be striking and unique – and it also allows for freedom of expression. By the use of brush marks and the application of the paint, it is possible to create light, shadow and a sense of movement and atmosphere.

The key to this style is the mixing of colours, tones and shades to create texture, depth and often a sense of realism:

1　We often paint directly onto the wall without sketching up the design first. This is risky, but can pay off, so long as the prep work is thorough and you have firmed up the design's composition and scale. Good prep work must include preliminary sketches on paper, colour sample sheets and relevant images to work from.

2　However, be open to allowing the design to evolve as you work. Painting directly onto the wall without sketching it on first can create more movement and fluidity to your mark making. Don't be scared of making mistakes. Remember, the beauty of paint is that you can always paint over it!

3　In order to build up a depth and richness of colour it can be useful to underpaint certain areas in a flat colour and then blend two to three colours on top.

4　Lots of tiny sample pots will give you small amounts of a wide range of different paint colours, and are easier to work with than many large pots.

5　In an abstract design the brush marks themselves can become a feature of the design and give a bold modern feel.

6　Some leaves in this style are better painted in one sweep. Load up a pointy size 6 to 8 brush with a dark green and a medium green. Angle the brush with each brush mark to vary the tone and spread the leaves. Start in one spot and sweep sideways, pulling up to create the point of the leaf.

7　Using a range of brushes is important to allow the design to come to life. For example, when creating large brushy areas or moments of fine detail.

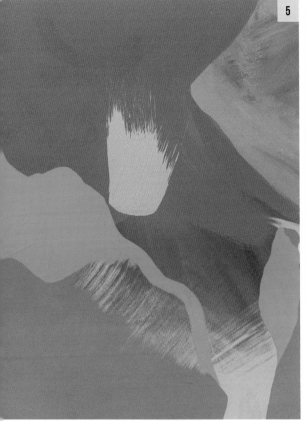

5

This style gives a more realistic three-dimensional effect.

6

7

IT MAY SEEM AS IF YOU WILL NEED LOTS OF PAINT FOR THIS STYLE OF PAINTING, BUT YOU'LL FIND THAT A SMALL AMOUNT OF PAINT ON YOUR BRUSH GOES A LONG WAY. SAMPLE POTS ARE OFTEN SUFFICIENT AND ALLOW YOU TO INVEST IN A LARGER RANGE OF COLOURS IN A COST-EFFECTIVE WAY. AN ARRAY OF SMALL COLOUR POTS IS SIMILAR TO WORKING WITH A PALETTE FOR A CANVAS PAINTING – AND COLOURS THAT YOU MAY THINK AREN'T RELEVANT CAN BECOME JUST THE RIGHT SHADE FOR A PARTICULAR BIRD OR LEAF.

Preparation

It's important to ensure you have the best finish possible for your wall before you begin. The smoother the wall the easier the paint will glide on, resulting in fewer coats and an even finish. A rough wall creates little lumps under the surface of the paint, so your paintbrush gets caught and paint needs to be dabbed more often for coverage. This can get messy and takes a long time! A rough surface also affects the finished look of the mural – any tiny imperfections will catch the light and really stand out. You also need to prepare and protect the space you will be working in.

PREPARING INTERIOR WALLS

The existing paint quality on the wall will also affect your process and results. A wall painted in low-quality emulsion (acrylic latex) can become absorbent, sucking away new paint so you will need more than one coat for coverage. This is time-consuming and can result in an unprofessional and inconsistent appearance. If the wall has been painted in a satin finish paint – for example, in a kitchen or bathroom – the mural paint might find it harder to adhere. In an ideal world the wall will be newly plastered and painted by a professional decorator with an undercoat, plus two layers of top-quality wall emulsion.

MATERIALS AND TOOLS

Dust sheet (drop cloth)

Masking (low-stick) tape

Emulsion (acrylic latex) mist coat (optional)

Pliers

Filler

Putty knife

Ladder (if necessary)

Sanding block

Sandpaper in rough and fine grits

Vacuum cleaner

Bucket of water

Soap or heavy-duty all-purpose cleaner

Sponge or scrubbing brush if necessary

Roller

Base emulsion (acrylic latex)

> IF THE WALL IS BEING PREPARED FOR YOU BY DECORATORS, MAKE SURE THEY HAVE COLOUR-MATCHED YOUR CHOSEN BASE COLOUR AND APPLIED THIS – THEN YOUR BASE MURAL COLOUR WILL BE READY TO WORK ONTO.

1   Freshly plastered walls need to be touch dry, or the paint will trap moisture resulting in damp issues and the top coat not adhering correctly. Freshly painted walls also need plenty of time to dry thoroughly. The length of time depends on the room temperature, but we recommend at least two weeks for a warm heated room.

2   Spread out a good quality dust sheet (drop cloth) along the floor under your chosen wall. Tape up areas that need protecting, such as light switches and sockets. Tape over cornicing and skirting boards (baseboards).

3   New plaster needs a mist coat of watered down emulsion paint to be absorbed into the plaster as a stable base primer. Leave the mist coat to dry for at least 24 hours. A good way to test it is to apply a strip of masking tape – if it peels away without removing paint, your wall is ready for the top coat. It's particularly important to follow Steps 1 and 3 for designs that need taping, otherwise pulling away the tape can remove entire chunks of paint exposing fresh plaster beneath.

4   If your wall is already smooth, then jump to Step 5. Remove nails, screws or hooks with a pair of pliers and fill holes with quick-drying filler using a putty knife. Fill three times – allowing to dry between each application because the compound shrinks when it dries. Sand between each application. Give a final sand using a fine grit paper and block over each former blemish. Check the wall for imperfections and vacuum up any dust.

5 Paint goes onto a wall best when it is not dusty or dirty. Get your bucket, sponge and soap and gently wipe down the entire wall surface. For stubborn stains you can use a heavier duty all-purpose cleaner and scrub!

6 If the wall has been prepared by a decorator, skip Steps 6 and 7. Once the wall is clean and dry it's time to apply a base coat, such as good-quality flat latex primer. If there are lots of marks you could use a stain-blocking primer instead – this will work similar to a base coat.

7 Let the primer layer dry before using your roller to apply two coats of your mural base coat emulsion. When choosing paint types please refer to Paint: Indoor Paint.

8 Before beginning to paint the final design, clear the area and set up as described in Preparation: Preparing the Space.

PREPARING EXTERIOR WALLS

The prepared surface of your exterior wall is also vital to the success of your mural. Don't just turn up to an outside wall with a can of paint and start painting! Paint will not adhere for long to a wall that is dirty, greasy or has old paint flaking away. Unless you are working on a newly-rendered exterior wall it is quite likely that you will need to prepare your surface beforehand. An exterior wall surface is likely to be rendered brick, brick, timber or stone.

MATERIALS AND TOOLS

Pressure washer (optional)

Scrubbing brush

Bucket of hot soapy water

Specialist cleaning products (if necessary)

Ladder (if necessary)

Stabilizing primer

Paint tray

Large flat paintbrush

1 If it is a large wall and you have the means, then a pressure washer (the type you use for driveways) can be used. These can be hired from most DIY shops (hardware stores). If it's a smaller wall, then use a scrubbing brush to clean the wall with hot soapy water. If you have stubborn marks or green algae growth you can use a specialist cleaning product (see Suppliers). Make sure the wall is thoroughly dry.

2 Next apply a stabilizing primer to your wall, which works like a base coat. This step is vital for the longevity of your mural. Use a large flat brush and tray and apply one coat from top to bottom; we like using Polyvine Clear Primer, which can be used on most exterior surfaces.

3 An interior wall may also be brick, in which case you may treat it as an exterior wall.

PREPARING THE SPACE

When you are ready to begin painting your mural design, whether it is inside or outside, you will need to prepare the site first. Spread a clean dust sheet (drop cloth) under the wall and mask any areas that need it with tape. Remove any furniture that is obstructing access to the wall. Lay out your brushes, paint pots and glass jars filled with water. Lay down a wad of kitchen paper towel and J Cloth, for dab-drying the brush after rinsing – your paintbrush needs to be as dry as possible when painting, especially when using tape. If working to a specific design have this to hand, from your sketchbook or your chosen image.

SCALING UP: PROJECTOR METHOD

If your mural design is detailed it's important to scale it up appropriately on the wall. One option is to use a projector, then trace the design over the projection directly onto the wall with paints or chalk. You could use the projector to draw in key aspects of the design and then work freehand on the rest. You will need to consider the light: if working inside you will need to make the room dark; if working outside you will need to wait until it gets dark. You may need to prop the projector up at different levels to get the image in the right place.

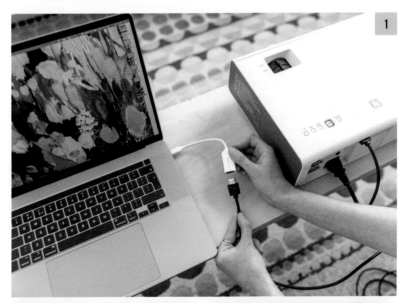

MATERIALS AND TOOLS

Projector

Extension lead (if necessary)

Laptop with design image to project

2H pencil

1 Link the projector to the laptop that has the chosen image. Turn on the projector and turn off all the lights.

2 Move your projector higher or lower, or further back or forward, until you have generated the correct size image for your wall.

3 Sketch the design lightly onto the wall using a 2H pencil.

4 Sometimes the edges of the design get skewed on a projection, so keep referring back to the original image.

DON'T WORRY ABOUT FILLING IN EVERY DETAIL. YOU ARE USING THE PROJECTION AS A GUIDE FOR SIZE AND COMPOSITION. DETAILS CAN BE ADDED IN LATER.

SCALING UP: GRID METHOD

Using a grid to scale your artwork is the most common method used by muralists. Although we tend to sketch our designs directly onto the wall freehand, we like using this technique as a visual check once we have completed our designs. Sometimes seeing the grid drawn over a design exposes areas that potentially might not work when translated onto a wall. It's also a fail-safe way to manage to stay within scale and it's easy-peasy.

MATERIALS AND TOOLS

Sketchbook/A4 sheet of paper

Mural design

Ruler

Pencil

Tape measure or long ruler

Posca pen or pencil

Ladder (if necessary)

1 Draw your mural design on a sheet of A4 or A3 paper or in your sketchbook. Use a ruler and pencil to draw a grid over it. Think about how big your wall is in relation to the grid, because the grid relates to the size of the wall and each square represents a measurement of your choice. Most common is 1 x 1m (3 x 3ft), so if you have a 3 x 3m (9 x 9ft) wall, you could use a grid with three rows and three columns of squares. All you need to worry about is accurately measuring the wall height and length and making sure the grid lines are spaced accurately and evenly on your paper.

2 Now draw a grid of squares with a pencil on your wall that mimics the grid of your sketch – so you will have the same number and arrangement of squares as on your mural design, but drawn on the wall at a much larger size. You can use a ruler or a rough line to mark the squares.

3 In each square of your mural draw the section of your design that corresponds to that square in your sketch. Work from the left of the wall to the right and link up the lines from each grid.

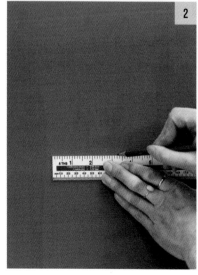

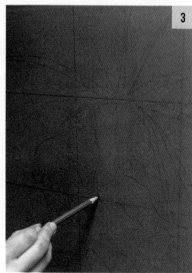

SCALING UP: DOODLE GRID METHOD

This is essentially an advanced version of the grid method and is particularly useful for very large walls of 12m (39ft) in length or more. As the name implies you will use doodles drawn onto the wall, plus an app called Procreate – or you can use Photoshop, if this is more familiar.

MATERIALS AND TOOLS

Sketchbook/A4 sheet of paper

Mural design

Pencil

Tablet or mobile phone (cell phone)

Procreate app or Photoshop

Posca pen or water-based crayon

Ladder

1   Sketch out on paper the rough shape of your chosen wall, adding any details such as windows. On top of this add your mural design. You can use collages, cut-out shapes, or shapes from our Templates. You can go as detailed as you like here, painting in colour or just outlines, as close to your final design as you can.

2   Take a photo of your mural design on your tablet or phone. Open up the Procreate app on your tablet and either download the photo of your mural design into the app or drop from your photos onto the app page.

3   This is the fun part! Take a Posca pen or water-based crayon and get your ladder out. Start drawing doodles around the wall – circles, shapes, letters, numbers anything goes! Leave space between each doodle of about 30cm (12in). Don't worry about neatness or style, because it will all be painted over.

4   Using your tablet or phone, take a photograph of your wall – doodles and all. Make sure you position your phone as straight on as possible horizontally (landscape) so that you capture the entire wall in one photo. If the wall is very wide you could split the design into two sections and think of it as two murals, taking two photos.

5   Open up your Procreate app or Photoshop and download the photograph of the wall into the app/software. Open up the photograph of your sketched-out wall and move this to the Procreate folder. Then follow the instructions on the app/software to superimpose your mural design onto the doodled wall. You will first need to 'fade' the photograph of your mural design. Then when you merge this photograph on top of the photograph of your doodled wall, the doodle marks will show through.

6   Either print out the merged photographic image of your wall or work directly from your device. Starting in the top left corner of your wall, use a pencil to draw in a component of your design that intersects the top left doodle on your wall. This doesn't need to be completely accurate, but as close as possible.

7   Keep working your way across your design section by section, as with the grid method. The difference here is that the doodles are your guide not the lines of a grid. It is important to continuously stand back and assess progress. Also vital is that you work section by section, from left to right and back again down the wall – this helps things stay accurate.

Projects

By now we hope you have a better understanding of the preparatory stages of mural making. Hopefully you have a wall in mind, have collated images and colour samples, sketched out a design and gathered together the painting equipment you will need. You are ready to begin! In this section we look in detail at ten murals in the three basic mural styles we use for our work. Some of our mural techniques are more complex than others and involve a greater level of painting experience, so each project has a skill level. If you are new to painting or less confident, then either begin with a one-roller mural or practise ahead of time. We often practise techniques on either a small section of wall, or on a large canvas (1m/3ft square). Both these options can easily be repainted to begin again!

CHINOISERIE-STYLE CHERRY TREE

Chinoiserie might seem a daunting style of mural painting, but if you follow these simple steps you can replicate this beautiful style of wallpaper. Preparation is key here – good imagery and practise sketches are vital. You really need to get a feel for the wiggly trunk, branches and leaves before launching onto a wall. For imagery, check out Pinterest. There are also lots of wallpaper companies that you can get inspiration from – for example, De Gournay or Milton & King. If you feel more confident, perhaps use a real-life photograph of a cherry tree to work from or sketch from life. Experiment with colours – dab sample paints onto watercolour paper, and mix colours up to see what sings for you.

SKILL LEVEL:

WE LOVE CRAIG & ROSE METALLIC COLOURS FOR OUR CHINOISERIE. THEIR BRONZE GOLD, ANTIQUE GOLD AND ROSE GOLD PAINTS LOOK STUNNING WHEN MIXED WITH FLATTER COLOURS AND WILL BRING A DEPTH AND SHINE. THINK BROWNS, GOLDS, SILVERS FOR THE TRUNK AND BRANCHES. PINKS, ORANGES, SILVERS AND WHITES FOR THE BLOSSOM. GREENS, ORANGES, GOLD, YELLOWS AND BLUES FOR THE LEAVES.

Materials and tools

PREP WORK:

- Roll of lining paper
- Pencil
- Masking (low-stick) tape
- Imagery printouts – the tree, leaves, blossom
- Sketchbook or paper
- Colour sample sheet

PAINTING THE MURAL:

- Dust sheet (drop cloth)
- Stepladder
- 2H or 3H pencil
- Selection of Chinoiserie brushes
- Selection of painting brushes between sizes 4 to 20 in mixed shapes: pointed rounds, blunt rounds, flat and filbert
- Two large glass jars of water to clean brushes
- Roll of paper towel and two J Cloths
- Sample pots of paint: at least three greens, light brown, dark brown, gold, silver, pink, yellow, red and white

Step 1

PRACTISING THE SHAPES AND LEAVES

Wall lining paper is excellent here – you can roll it out on the floor and copy out the length of the tree shape in pencil, experimenting with leaves and branches. We always draw freehand onto the wall, but you may find it easier to print out enlarged sections of trunk and branches. Using the lining paper as a template, you can cut out your tree and tape it to the wall as a simple stencil. If you plan to draw freehand onto the wall, this is your chance to practise getting a feel for the tree shapes – noticing, for example, how bumpy and irregular the cherry branches are. This is an important feature when trying to make the tree look realistic.

Step 2

PENCILLING YOUR DESIGN ONTO THE WALL

Either draw or stencil the trunk of the cherry tree and the branches onto the wall. Be as light handed and 'loose' as you can be. It's ok to make mistakes – you can rub these out and try again. Focus on the main form to begin with; the trunk followed by the branches and leaves in descending order of size. Don't worry about the bumps and grooves in the trunk and branches – you can add these later. Use a light pencil – 2H or 3H.

Step 3

PAINTING THE TRUNK

Using a filbert brush size 20, work your way up the trunk filling the shape as you go. Then load a medium-size flat or round brush, size 16 to 18, with two colours to begin with – brown and gold/yellow. To capture the spherical shape of the trunk make sure the darker brown is along one edge, with a gold or beige colour toward the other side to mimic the light. Try to think random: the key to a cherry tree is the nobbly curved edges and bumps. It has few straight edges!

Step 4

PAINTING THE MEDIUM SIZE BRANCHES

Load up a medium-size pointed paintbrush, size 10 to 12, with silver or shimmery white gold. Paint all the branches, using smaller paintbrushes as you work your way to the slimmer branches (see Technical Painting Styles: Painterly Style, Step 6).

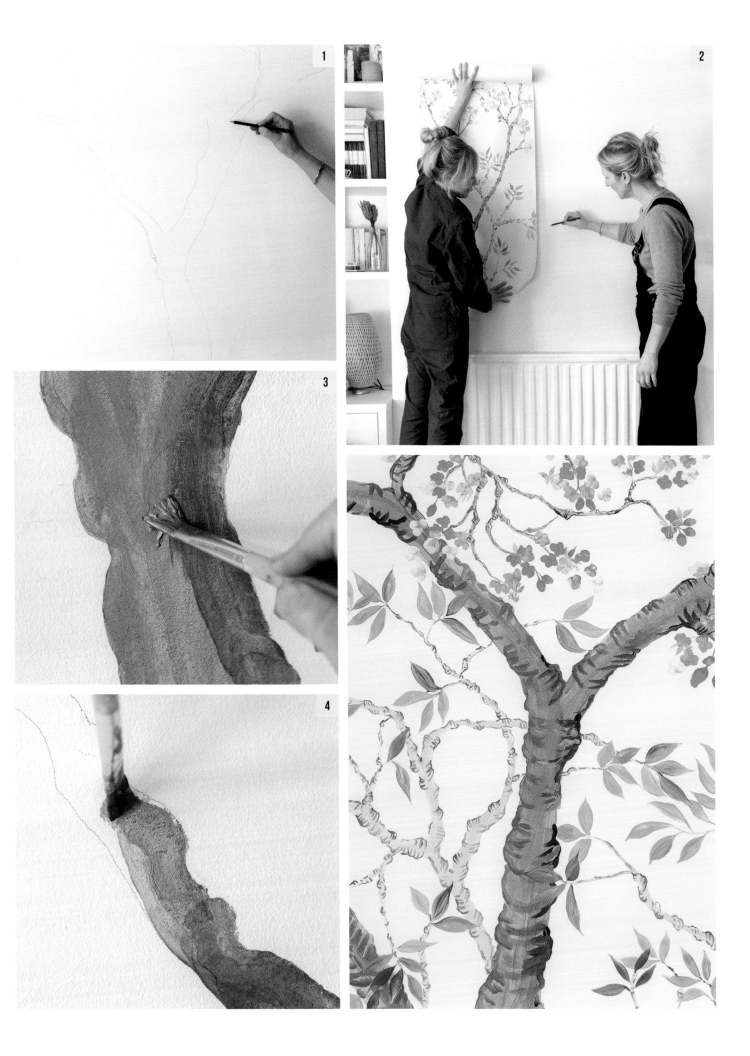

5

 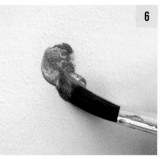

6

 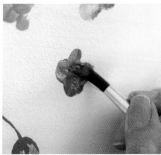

7

STRUCTURALLY BLOSSOM COMES HIGHER UP
THE TREE SO FOCUS ON YOUR TOP BRANCHES.
IF YOU HAVE THE CONFIDENCE WE RECOMMEND
GOING STRAIGHT ONTO THE WALL WITH PAINT
(AFTER EXPERIMENTING ON PAPER). DRAWING UP
THE SHAPES FIRST WOULD BE TIME CONSUMING
AND THE RESULT LESS EXCITING. PLACE BLOSSOM
FLOWERS IN GROUPS OF FIVE OR SIX, RANDOMLY
SCATTERED ABOUT THE BRANCHES. AT THIS STAGE
THEY 'FLOAT' APART FROM THE BRANCHES –
CONNECTIVE STALKS COME LATER.

8

Step 5

PAINTING THE LINES OF THE BARK

Load a fine, pointed brush with dark brown paint and slowly, using semi-circular strokes, work up the trunk from the ground upward. Next, using a similar brush, work vertically along the edge of the trunk, creating bumps along the way. Finally, using a lighter brown and a small size pointy brush, do the same along the silvery branches. Be delicate. Leave out patches or sections – you can always return. Less is more here.

Step 6

PAINTING BLOSSOMS

Using a rounded soft paintbrush, size 6 to 8, dab half the brush into the white and half into the pink. Using a light motion dab four dots together to create each blossom flower. With each dab press down and swirl the brush on the spot before releasing to leave a circular swirl. You can choose whether to tilt the brush, allowing more pink or more white to vary the tone of each flower. For the little green leaves attached to each blossom, use the same technique, this time using a small, pointed brush, dabbing yellow and green and flicking up the ends to make a pointed leaf shape.

Step 7

PAINTING SLENDER STALKS AND STRAGGLY BITS READY FOR LEAVES

Using silver or gold mixed with a light brown, use the tip of a thin pointy brush, size 4 to 6, to paint thin bendy lines all over the ends of the branches. Aim toward the groups of blossoms. Lower down the tree create your only family of branches, getting smaller and more 'flicky' toward the end of each branch.

Step 8

LAYERING THE LEAVES

The lower branches of the tree will have the leaves. This part of the tree takes a long time and needs patience. Start in each section and work your way around the branches. Using a pointy size 6 to 8 brush, load up dark green and medium green. Angle the brush with each brush mark to vary the tone. Spread the leaves in bunches of six. Paint each leaf with one sweep in a similar way to the blossom, only this time you are starting in one spot and sweeping sideways pulling up to create a point. Sometimes the leaves take on a style of their own so watch out – you are aiming for long and pointy, not fat and very curved. The leaves are very particular on a cherry tree.

MESSY BRUSH STROKES MURAL

This is a mural you can really have some fun with! A mixture of blocks of colour, abstract shapes and brushy sweeps – this is one mural not to hold back on. Layering is key to this design, and the bold palette makes it truly come alive. Colours can be changed to suit your space, but make sure you take some time to consider how they work together. The beauty of this mural is in the sense of spontaneity; the odd random shape or drip can add to the overall effect. The mural that best demonstrates this technique is one we painted for a sushi restaurant in Brighton. We have chosen a section of this mural minus the lettering to show the technique.

SKILL LEVEL:

WE HAVE USED FARROW & BALL MIDDLETON PINK FOR THE BACKGROUND, ALONG WITH VERDIGRIS GREEN (DARK GREEN) AND ARSENIC (TURQUOISE), AS WELL AS CRAIG & ROSE FLEURIE (BLUE/GREEN) AND LAMPLIGHTER (YELLOW) IN THIS MURAL.

Materials and tools

PREP WORK:

- Dust sheet (drop cloth)
- Stepladder
- Two small rollers and tray (if painting the base coat yourself)
- Pale pink emulsion (acrylic latex)
- 2H pencil
- Templates – lotus flower, rose
- Colour sample sheet

PAINTING THE MURAL:

- Several 2cm (0.75in) and 2.5cm (1in) angled decorators' brushes
- Selection of large round brushes in sizes 10 to 14
- Filbert brushes in sizes 14 and 16
- Roll of paper towel and J Cloth
- Several large glass jars of water to clean brushes
- Selection of paints in dark green, light grey, red, hot pink, purple, white, orange, turquoise, blue/green, yellow
- Fat decorators' brush approx 15–18cm (6–7in) wide
- White PC-7M Posca pen

Step 1
PREPARING THE WALL

Begin by painting the entire wall in the background colour – here we have used pale pink. Ideally use a professional decorator to give you a good finish. If this is not possible then see Preparing the Wall: Preparing Interior Walls and follow the steps for preparation and base coat coverage. You will need to use a roller and will need to paint at least two coats for a deeper hue.

Step 2
SCALING UP THE DESIGN

Choose a scaling up method of your choice – see Preparation: Scaling Up for the various options. We used doodle grid for this mural because the doodles will be covered by the design. Using whichever scaling up technique you have chosen, draw up the main lines of the design onto the wall using a 2H pencil.

Step 3
BLOCKING IN THE FIRST SHAPES

Using an angled decorators' brush, block in the dark green shapes first. Use a large flat brush for quick and easy coverage of the larger areas and then swap to a pointed round for any finer edges. In some places the shape is swept to a fine point.

Step 4
ADDING SECOND SHAPES

Next add the light grey shapes, being careful to create a clean edge next to the green. Again, use a large flat brush such as the angled decorators' brush for the large areas and then swap to a pointed round brush where necessary for more detail.

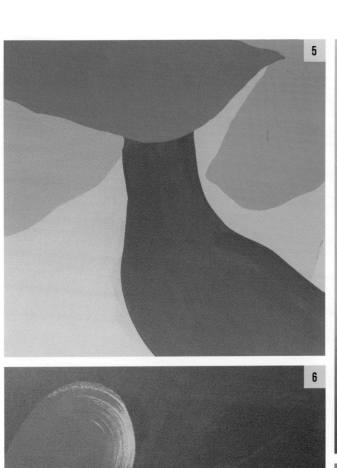

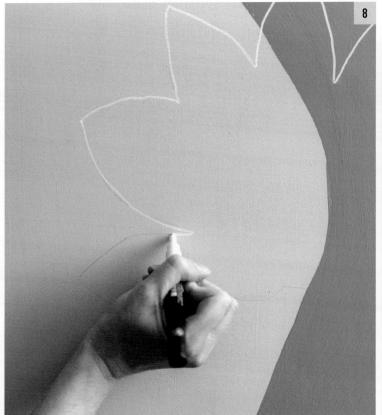

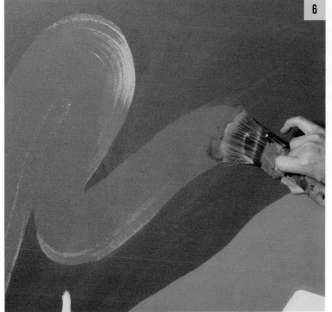

Step 5

FILLING IN THE REMAINING SHAPES

Work your way across the wall, filling in the shapes from larger to smaller until the wall is completely covered.

Step 6

ADDING MESSY BRUSH STROKES

Now for the fun part. Take the 15–18cm (6–7in) wide decorators' brush, fill with red paint and sweep in flowing curving shapes over the top of your painted shapes. You might need to reload halfway through. Don't worry about this; let your entire body sweep around with you. It's a whole body movement, so let yourself feel expressive and flow. The more you go for it, the more dramatic the result will be. If you make a mistake, remember our mantra – you can always paint over! You can repeat this process with other colours over the wall if you wish.

Step 7

DRAWING IN THE LINEAR FLOWERS

Choose one of the linear flower designs from the Template section – either the lotus flower or the rose. Hold your flower template up to the wall and draw around it with your pencil.

Step 8

FINISHING THE LINEAR FLOWERS

Removing the template, take a fat white Posca PC-7M pen and draw over the lines of the flower – if you prefer you can use a slimmer profile pen, this is up to you. You will need to draw each line two or three times so they will shine through. Alternatively, you could use a gold Posca or any colour of your choice so long as the lines make an impact over the painted wall behind.

ABSTRACT GEOMETRIC MURAL

A graphic mural design is great fun and a good chance to express yourself within some helpful boundaries. Remember you can choose any design you like, but to get you started we have chosen a classic design that never fails. It involves basic primary shapes of differing sizes layered up and juxtaposed with strong lines on top. This mural can be as complex as you dare or very simple. During each step, there are chances for you to expand the design in scale or with the quantity of shapes you add. Whilst you will only be 'blocking' in shapes with colour, the simplicity of the shapes means they need to be executed beautifully. This means attention to precise edging and a couple of paint layers for an opaque finish.

SKILL LEVEL:

USE UP THE LEFTOVERS. INSTEAD OF BUYING LOTS OF SAMPLE POTS FOR A MURAL LIKE THIS, YOU COULD USE LEFTOVER HOUSEHOLD EMULSIONS (LATEX PAINT).

Materials and tools

PREP WORK:

- Pencil
- String
- Sticky tape
- Selection of household stencils and templates: for circles we use plates, serving dishes, mugs, cookie cutters and any other shapely objects you fancy using

PAINTING THE MURAL:

- Dust sheet (drop cloth)
- Stepladder
- Selection of painting brushes between sizes 8 to 10 in mixed shapes: pointed rounds, blunt rounds, flat and filbert
- 2cm (0.75in) and 2.5cm (1in) angled decorators' brushes
- Several large glass jars of water to clean brushes
- Roll of paper towel and a J Cloth
- Sample pots of paint in your chosen colours
- Masking (low-stick) tape

Step 1

DRAWING THE LARGE CIRCLE

We like to draw a large base shape on the wall to get things going. This acts as an anchor for the design and from here you can expand. If you have a different design in mind that utilizes only smaller shapes, then skip to Step 2. Using a pencil, mark a spot on the wall as the centre of your circle; we suggest mid wall at eye level. Cut a length of string about 60cm (24in) long and tape one end securely to a pencil. Ask your assistant to hold the other end of the string firmly to your mark on the wall. From this point, gently stretch out the string until it is taut and, holding the pencil at right angles to the wall, draw the first half of the circle on one side. Swap sides with your assistant and repeat to draw the second half of the circle.

IT'S OK TO ASK FOR HELP. YOU MAY NEED AN ASSISTANT ON THE OTHER END OF THE STRING IF YOU ARE USING THE STRING AND PENCIL METHOD TO DRAW A LARGE CIRCLE.

Step 2

ADDING SMALLER BASE CIRCLES

Hold the largest circular dish on the wall overlapping your large circle, then draw around it. Use different size circles/templates to add more to the design – you can fan out circles into smaller shapes, or overlap everywhere. Feel free to express yourself. You can always rub out.

Step 3

PAINTING THE BASE CIRCLES

Choose three or four colours to start with – if you have more colours you can add these later. Paint the biggest shapes first. The big base circle can be painted in one colour, the smaller circles a mixture of colours – you decide!

Step 4

OVERLAPPING THE BASE CIRCLES

Notice where your smaller circles overlap other shapes; you can choose to either paint one shape completely overlapping the other – or a fun way to work this is to choose another paint colour for the intersection, as in a coloured Venn diagram.

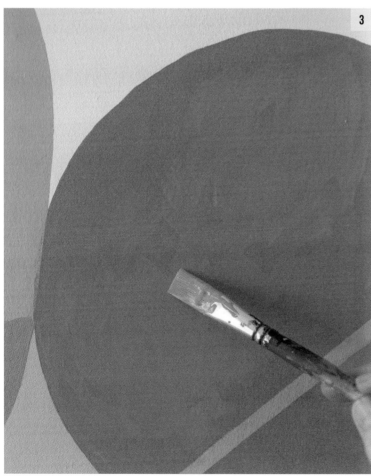

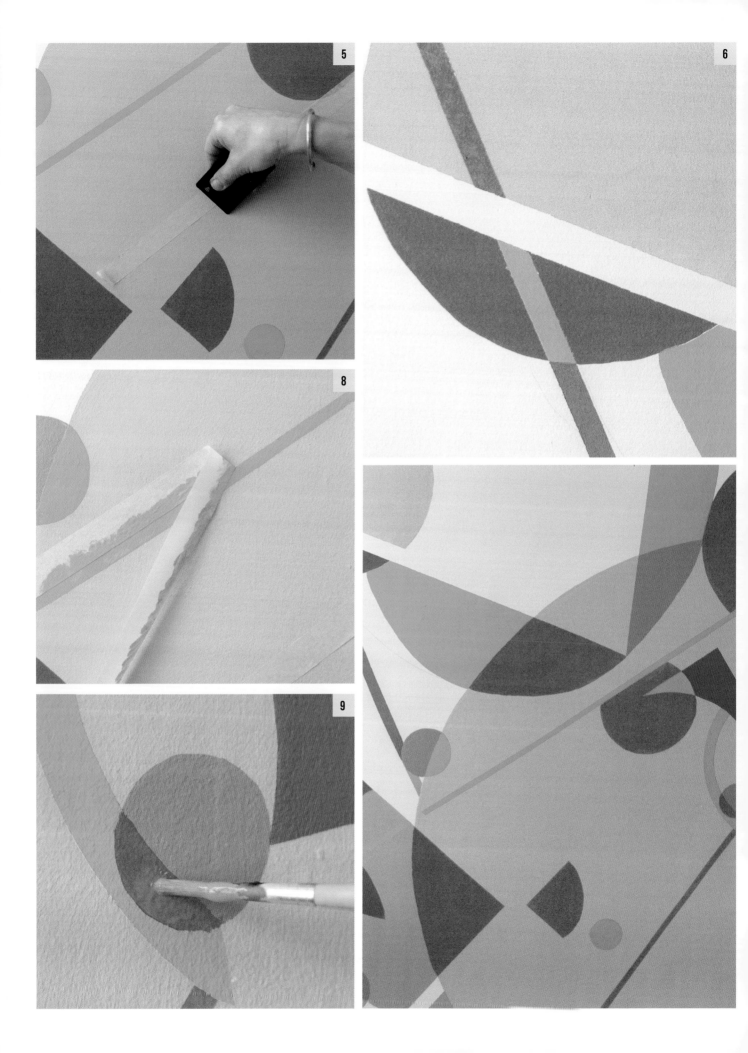

Step 5
ADDING STRAIGHT-LINE SHAPES

Stick one end of tape in the middle of your giant circle and roll it out to your desired length, smoothing it out as you go. You can repeat this process in other areas of the wall, fanning outward from the central circle or coming in at jaunty angles from the corners of the wall toward the centre. You can create right angle corners or triangles with your tape or keep the lines in uniform stripes – the choices are endless! You can choose the width of the gap: 10cm (4in) works well for slim lines or go wider if you like.

Step 6
PAINTING IN STRAIGHT LINES AND ANGULAR SHAPES

As with Step 4, you can choose to paint these lines in totally so they overlap the circles beneath, or you can leave the intersections to be painted in separate colours before or after you have removed the tape. When painting, follow the technique described in Technical Painting Styles: Flat Graphic Style, Step 5.

Step 7
ADDING A SECOND COAT

Once you have filled in all the shapes, work your way around once more. Two coats of paint might not be necessary everywhere, but for overlaps this is often needed.

Step 8
PEELING OFF THE TAPE

It's a good idea to take the tape off once you are happy with your paintwork. To avoid taking off more paint than you want, slowly and very gently peel backward in the direction you are peeling (see Technical Painting Styles: Flat Graphic Style, Step 6).

Step 9
TOUCHING UP

Once all of the tape is off, you can stand back and admire your handiwork. It's inevitable that there will be imperfections or small areas that the tape has taken a little bit more paint off than it should have. There might be some bleeding in places. Just use a flat head brush, size 8 or 10, and work your way around the wall to touch up spots. It's time consuming but makes a big difference. Well done!

DARK BACKGROUND MURAL

A mural with a dark background can bring a wonderful warmth and richness to your home, and here we guide you through painting a glamorous mural with a maximalist feel. By following the simple steps you will find that the bright colours glow on the black backdrop. In this mural we use orange blossom, rose hips, camellia, geraniums and echium to create a beautiful botanical design. However, you can swap these plants for any you prefer, to create your own personal mural. We have used species that vary in colour and shape, growing from above and below. You can play with this composition to suit your space.

SKILL LEVEL: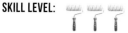

WE HAVE USED FARROW & BALL RAILINGS (BLACK) FOR THE BACKGROUND OF OUR MURAL, WITH FOLIAGE AND FLOWERS IN PAINT & PAPER LIBRARY HUNTER DUNN (DARK GREEN), FARROW & BALL ARSENIC (MEDIUM GREEN), AND LITTLE GREENE PAINT IN THEATRE RED (DEEP RED), MARIGOLD (ORANGE) AND PALE LUPIN (LILAC BLUE).

Materials and tools

PREP WORK:

- Dust sheet (drop cloth)
- Stepladder
- Two small rollers and tray (if painting the base coat yourself)
- Black emulsion (acrylic latex)
- Roll of lining paper
- Pencil
- Templates – camellia leaves, orange blossom and orange blossom leaves, rose hip leaves and fruit, geranium leaves and flowers (or other plants of your choice)
- Sketchbook or paper
- Colour sample sheet

PAINTING THE MURAL:

- Selection of paintbrushes between sizes 4 to 18 in mixed shapes: pointed rounds, blunt rounds and flat
- Two large glass jars of water to clean brushes
- Roll of paper towel and two J Cloths
- Sample pots of paint: dark green, medium green, white, pink, deep pink, yellow ochre, brown, deep red, orange, lilac blue

Step 1

PREPARING THE WALL

Begin by painting the entire mural area in black – see Preparing the Wall: Preparing Interior Walls and follow the steps for preparation and base coat coverage. You will need to use a roller and will need to paint two coats for a deeper hue.

Step 2

PRACTISING THE SHAPES AND LEAVES

Roll the lining paper out on the floor and map out the composition of the mural, experimenting with the shape and size of the fruits and foliage. You might find it easier to stencil on some of the shapes, see Templates section. If you plan to draw the design freehand this is your chance to practise getting a feel for the different leaf shapes. Think about varying the sizes, keeping wiggly edges and twisty stems.

Step 3

PENCILLING THE CAMELLIA LEAVES AND FLOWER ONTO THE WALL

Either draw or stencil the large camellia leaves onto the wall. Remember to overlap the leaf shapes, keep the stem bumpy and be sure to include leaf buds. In our design we have supersized the camellia as a backdrop for the rest of the mural. These leaves are not grounded but meander over the wall to create depth. Finally draw in the camellia flowers – two to three larger flowers and four to five buds. Keep the shape loose and blousy; there is no need to draw in any detail, just a rough wiggly circular shape. You can use photographs of camellias as reference.

Step 4

PAINTING THE CAMELLIA LEAVES

For the leaves and stem choose a darker and lighter green. Load a medium-size flat brush with the darker green and paint half your first leaf in this colour. Clean your brush and dab on some of the lighter green, overlapping with the dark. Using a dry, clean medium-size flat brush, blend the two colours together, working from the centre toward the outside of the leaf. Repeat with each leaf. For the stem, use a size 6 to 8 pointed round brush.

Step 5

PAINTING THE CAMELLIA FLOWERS

We recommend practising this in advance on some paper. Load up a medium-size flat brush with mainly white paint, along with a tiny touch of pink. Swirl the paint in circular motions to create the effect of overlapping petals. Using a size 6 pointed round brush, swirl through some moments of darker pink in thin lines, circling the centre of the flower. You may want to introduce a touch of yellow, blended with the white to create depth. Keep your brush marks loose. Repeat for each of the flowers and allow to dry.

Step 6

DRAWING ORANGES AND STEMS AND PAINTING THE LEAVES

Begin to pencil in the orange blossom stems, which trail from the top of the wall. Start by drawing in the oranges; if you find it hard to draw freehand, use a small bowl or plate to draw round. We drew two oranges disappearing off the edge to give the mural a more expansive feel. Once you have positioned the oranges, draw a trailing single pencil line to act as a branch. Keep the line loose and meandering. We tend to paint the leaves straight onto the wall for spontaneity and movement in the design. If you feel nervous, draw the leaf in first instead. Remember to place some of the leaves going behind the oranges.

Step 7

ADDING THE ORANGE BLOSSOM FLOWERS

The orange blossom itself is also more effective if painted directly onto the wall without sketching, but you will also find it in the Templates section. The blossom is essentially six pronged petals in teardrop shapes, with the occasional, interspersed lone petal. Using a size 6 pointed round brush, working from the centre, sweep in each petal individually in white paint; again vary the sizes.

Step 8

PENCILLING THE ROSE HIPS

The rose hips trail in from the side of the wall and their leaves are a much fuller shape than the orange blossom leaves. Twist and turn them to overlap with the large camellia leaves and orange blossom leaves, either using the stencil provided or by drawing freehand. Once again, painting directly onto the wall without pencilling can give terrific movement. The rose hips should be a similar size to the leaves and oval in shape. Cluster them in groups of two or three.

Step 9

PAINTING THE ROSE HIPS AND LEAVES

Start by painting in the branches. Dip a size 4 to 6 thin pointy brush in water and dab with some paper towel. Load with yellow ochre or brown and sweep across the wall, keeping your line as fine as possible. Let the line meander, flicking off at the ends. In order to make the rose hips as vibrant as possible, underpaint in white. Whilst drying, get to work on the leaves; their defining feature is their slightly serrated edges. Using two tones of green, work onto the wall using a size 8 to 10 pointed round brush. For the edges, swap to a size 4 to 6 point and sweep the paint to the edge of the leaf and into tiny points.

Step 10

ADDING DETAIL TO THE ROSE HIP LEAVES

Vary the light and dark leaf areas, always painting the background leaves in darker green. Once dried you can hint at veins using the same yellow ochre as the branches. This will require the smallest amount of paint on your brush. Keep the veins as thin as possible, never taking them as far as the edge of the leaf.

Step 11

FINISHING THE ROSE HIPS

Decide from what direction the light is falling onto the rose hips. Using a size 10 pointed round brush, fill in with deep red leaving a white circle where the light falls. Then using a dry, clean flat brush sweep a tiny amount of red from the edges over the white to blend. Insert a white dot on each rose hip as the highlight; you will have a juicy 3D rose hip. For the final touch, using a size 4 brush, add the spiky prongs to the bottom of the rose hips – these can be done in single sweeping movements ending in a point.

Step 12

UNDERPAINTING THE ORANGES

To make the oranges as vibrant as possible, start by underpainting them in white and allow to dry. Meanwhile, using the tip of a size 4 thin pointy brush, paint in the wiggly branches. Try to keep a steady hand and sweep in the lines – don't worry if some parts of the branch are slightly thicker than others. Now paint in each log and pointy leaf with one sweep (see Chinoiserie-style Cherry Tree: Step 8). Overlap some of the leaves and vary the sizes – variation in both colour and size is the key. Remember the leaves behind will be darker than the leaves painted over the top.

Step 13

PAINTING THE ORANGES

Using orange loaded onto a medium-size flat brush, sweep the colour in a circular movement round the edge of the orange and blend the colour toward the centre. Using a clean, dry brush swirl the brush over the painted area to create a blended light patch. This will give the impression of the orange being 3D. You may need to layer up around the outer edges of the orange in order to create density.

Step 14

FINISHING THE ORANGE BLOSSOM FLOWERS

To finish the orange blossom flowers, add an orange dot in the centre of each.

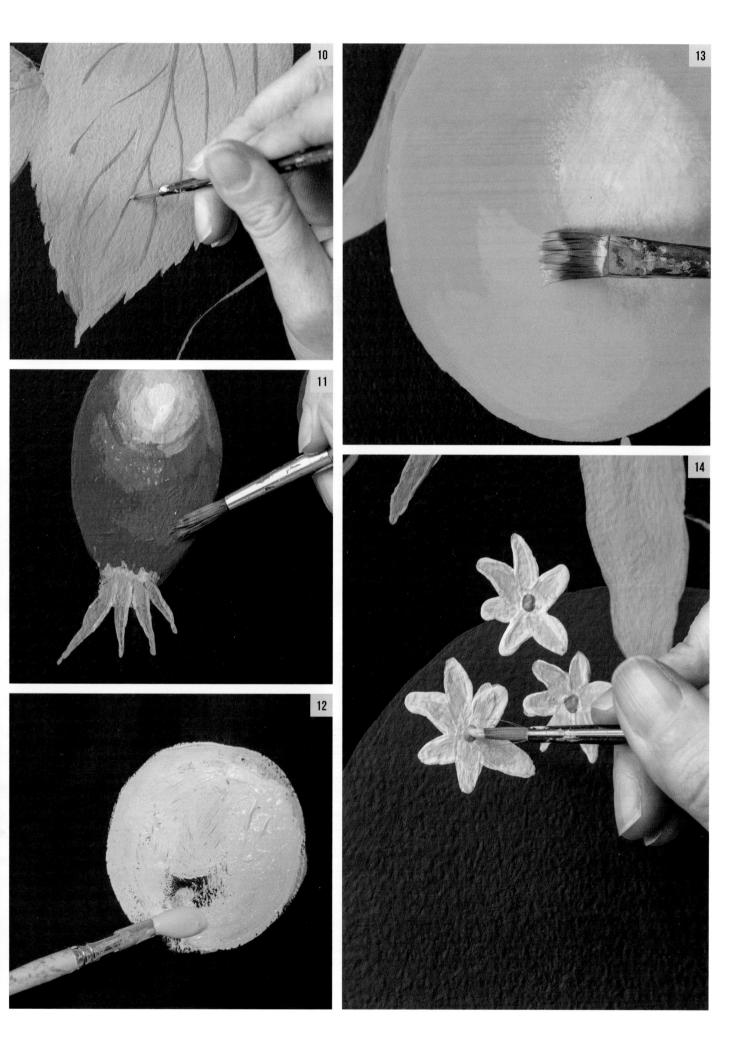

Step 15

PENCILLING THE GERANIUMS

Geraniums have wonderfully frilly round leaves. Keep your drawing loose and note the way leaves fold over. When painting this mural we brought some potted geraniums into the space from which to work. Again, stencils are provided if you prefer. The flowers themselves are made up of bunches of oval-shaped petals. The clusters of buds are important and add a playfulness. The stalks of a geranium are not wiggly but straight, sometimes a little bendy. Again, make sure you vary the shapes and sizes.

Step 16

PAINTING THE GERANIUMS

Load a size 8–10 pointed round brush with your two chosen greens. Here we use Farrow & Ball Arsenic which is a lovely zingy bluey green. Swoosh your paint around the leaf keeping it loose, adding in more of the darker green. Keep the edges frilly and lighter in places to give the impression of light hitting the leaf. You want your paint to be swirly and juicy. Next move on to the flowers. The petals should be underpainted in white and then pink dabbed on top with a size 6 pointed round brush. For the buds use the same approach, dabbing on the colour using green, moments of pink and just a touch of yellow.

Step 17

PENCILLING THE ECHIUM

The echium is an exotic tall plant which serves to ground the composition. Draw the stem, and portion each of the spiky leaves off the centre, overlapping and varying sizes. These work best painted directly onto the wall if you are confident enough. The flower is made up of lots of circles working their way into a point. Start by painting in the stem in one sweep (or as far as your loaded size 6 to 8 pointed round brush will go). Work each leaf off the stem in one sweep; for this, you will once again need to load your brush with two different greens. We have gone for a blue green and yellowy green.

Step 18

PAINTING THE ECHIUM FLOWER

Using a lilac blue colour paint, dab each circle individually. For the tiny spikes use the thinnest brush you have dipped with barely any paint on the end. Stroke tiny lines onto the edge of some of the circle using pale yellow. Dot the odd moment of green through the foliage.

EXTERIOR MURAL

An exterior mural is a wonderful way to bring life and colour to an old concrete or brick wall, but there are a few things that make painting an exterior more of a challenge than an interior. Firstly, you will need to consider the weather. Painting a mural in the rain is no fun and not very effective... trust us we know! Good preparation is key – you want your design to be able to withstand the elements for many years to come, so a well-prepared wall is essential to prevent flaking and deterioration of the paint. The design we have chosen here is very striking and bold, using graphic shapes. Given that exterior walls are often textured, you will find a graphic style with soft edges is most effective. We have created a sense of depth through layering, which can be achieved by following these steps. Make a statement with hot pinks and oranges!

SKILL LEVEL:

WE HAVE USED FARROW & BALL ARSENIC (MEDIUM GREEN) AND LITTLE GREENE PAINT MID AZURE GREEN (DARK GREEN) IN OUR MURAL.

Materials and tools

PREP WORK:

- Pencil
- Roll of lining paper
- Template – fig leaf
- Large flat brush
- Sample pot of paint
- Colour sample sheet
- Power washer (optional)
- Stabilizing primer
- Large flat paintbrush
- Dust sheet (drop cloth)
- Stepladder
- Roller
- Paint tray
- Light green masonry paint

PAINTING THE MURAL:

- Masonry paint: shades of light and dark green, pink, orange, white
- 2cm (0.75in) and 2.5cm (1in) angled mottler decorators' brushes
- Selection of paintbrushes in mixed shapes
- Tub of water to rinse brushes
- Roll of paper towel and two J Cloths

Step 1

PRACTISING THE BACKGROUND SHAPES

Start by practising the dark green layer of the mural on lining paper. We like to approach this freehand but it is worth working on the technique in advance. For this layer you are trying to give the impression of overlapping leaves and shadows, a feeling of dappled light. You can have fun with the shapes you create, blocking in and leaving gaps that reference leaves and seed heads. Make sure you leave a raggedy edge.

Step 2

PRACTISING THE FIG LEAVES

Take some time to practise drawing the shapes of fig leaves, which will be overlaid in pink and orange. Work from life or photos, or use the fig leaf in Templates as a starting point. You can also refer to the imagery you have collected in preparation for the mural, or you may like to choose other leaf shapes. The key is to keep these shapes varied in order to bring a sense of movement to the mural. Think about the composition of your mural and make some sketches. There is no need to follow the instructions here exactly if you would like to vary the design. For example, if your wall is very long, think about introducing some dark green along the top.

Step 3

PREPARING THE WALL AND APPLYING THE LIGHT GREEN BASE

Prepare the wall as outlined in Preparing the Wall: Preparing Exterior Walls. You will need to make sure it has been thoroughly cleaned, ideally with a power washer. All signs of organic growth must be removed. Once dry, paint on a layer of stabilizing primer. Do not apply if there is a risk of rain or if the air/surface temperature is likely to fall below 8°C (46°F). Allow to dry for no less than four hours. Paint the first layer of light green onto the wall – rollers are ideal for speedy coverage. Allow to dry and then paint over a second layer.

Step 4

ADDING THE DARK GREEN AREAS

Starting in the bottom corner of the wall, use your angled 2cm (0.75in) or 2.5cm (1in) brush to take your shapes to roughly half way across the wall. Sweep the shapes up the left-hand side of the wall, remembering to leave non uniformed gaps. Repeat this to the right of the wall. Allow to dry.

Step 5

DRAWING THE FIG LEAVES ON WALL

The fig leaves in pink and bright orange are really fun and juicy to paint. Draw them in with paint, using a medium-size or small 2cm (0.75in) angled decorators' brush. Try to keep your brush fairly dry, not loaded too heavily; if the paint is used quite sparsely at this stage it can easily be painted over if you make a mistake.

Step 6

PAINTING THE FIG LEAVES

Then block in the pink fig leaves – you will need a well-loaded brush or brushes at this point. For the middle of the leaves you can use a large flat brush, but for the outer edges make sure you have something with a point. It's important to keep those edges crisp, which can be challenging if the wall is bumpy. You might find that some dabbing is necessary to fill any awkward gaps. Allow to dry then repeat with overlapping orange fig leaves. Allow to dry.

Step 7

ADDING THE POINTY WHITE LEAVES

Using a fine-pointed round brush, load up with white paint and in one sweeping motion first draw on the stems, keeping the lines curving and arching. You may need to reload your brush mid-sweep but try and keep it as seamless as possible. Paint each leaf with one sweep, as shown in Technical Painting Styles: Painterly Style, Step 6. You are aiming for long and pointy, not fat and curved. Vary the spacing between leaves and remember to overlap some. We enjoy giving some of them a slightly broken edge and mixing up the sizes – you don't want uniformity here, there are never two leaves exactly the same. Even given this graphic style you can bring a painterly sensibility to it.

PAINTERLY BOTANICAL MURAL

A painterly botanical mural is a more traditional 'realistic' style of painting. The depth of the work in this style of mural can vary widely, from the oversized overlaying of three-dimensional plants and animals to tiny jewels of detail painted over flat graphic painted shapes. To demonstrate this technique we have chosen a fig leaf mural. This has two-layers: the base layer is the flat graphic shapes of fig leaves; the top layer is the complex painterly part, so it's a combination of 'graphic' and 'painterly botanical'. We have chosen it because it is a good starting point to practise this technique, which will take time, patience and a good deal of practise on paper first. But the finished affect has great depth, movement and drama.

SKILL LEVEL:

PREP WORK:

- Templates – fig leaf, birds (optional)
- Sketchbook or paper
- Pencil
- Roll of lining paper
- 2H or 3H pencil
- Colour sample sheet
- Camera or mobile phone (cell phone)
- Printer

PAINTING THE MURAL:

- Dust sheet (drop cloth)
- Stepladder
- Selection of brushes: round sizes 8 to 12, filbert sizes 16 and 20, pointed liner size 4
- Two large glass jars of water to clean brushes
- Roll of paper towel and two J Cloths
- Sample pots of paint: light blue-green, range of greens and blues, yellows, pinks, red, warm white

WE HAVE USED CRAIG & ROSE SUNG BLUE (LIGHT BLUE-GREEN), FLEURIE (DEEP BLUE-GREEN) AND CHINESE WHITE (WARM WHITE) IN OUR MURAL.

Step 1
DRAWING THE FIG LEAVES

The fig has a very specific style of leaf that is wonderful to paint. The key is to get the scale and wiggly edges correct. To do this, either gather together imagery of fig leaves and fig plants – or a real plant, if you have one – and have a go at copying them. Or you can cut out images or use the fig leaf shape in the Templates section. Practise drawing fig leaves on rolls of lining paper.

Step 2
WORKING OUT THE DESIGN

Take a photograph of your chosen wall and print it out, then sketch out your fig leaves – or one entire fig plant – onto your wall elevation. You can experiment with different layouts on multiple printouts; so draw out one option with the plant 'grounded' – rising from the ground – and draw another option with the leaves 'floating' in a more abstract manner across your wall. Your chosen design will form the first layer of your mural – the flat graphic background leaves. Use a scaling up technique of your choice to draw your design onto the wall (see Preparation for scaling up methods).

Step 3
PAINTING THE GRAPHIC FIG LEAVES

Choose a pale blue-green colour for the leaves. Using a size 12 round brush, fill each fig leaf shape with paint. Use a smaller size 8 to 10 round brush to neaten up each edge. Keep the paint as flat as possible – there should be no colour variation because this layer is supposed to be a graphic one-dimensional base. Let each layer dry before beginning the next. You will need at least two coats for this base. If you are painting onto a dark wall colour you will need to underpaint each leaf shape in white first.

Step 4
ADDING THE SECOND LAYER

Once the base layer has dried it is time to draw in the second layer. Using exactly the same process as the first layer, draw in more fig leaves and fruit across your wall.
This time it's important to consider the arrangement – make sure your fig leaves are random and show gaps of wall, and these leaves will overlap the graphic leaves so make sure the graphic leaves are exposed in large areas.

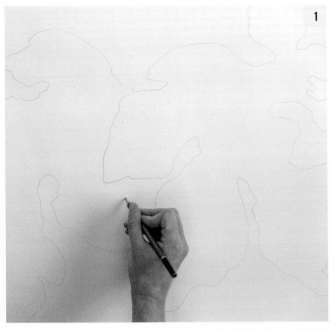

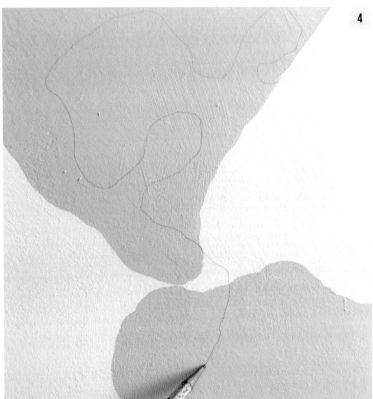

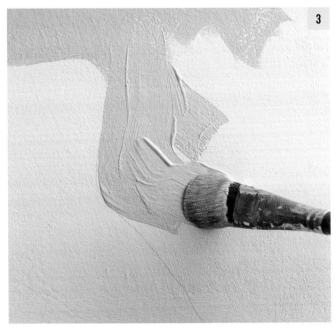

Step 5

PAINTING THE PAINTERLY LAYER OF FIG LEAVES

Lay out the paint colours for the top layer; for the leaves, dark green, light green, yellow and a soft muted blue-green; for the fig fruit, dark red, orange, pink yellow and white. Taking a medium to large filbert size 20, quickly fill in the leaves in a mixture of pale yellow and blue-green. You can do this randomly as a quick base coat.

Step 6

ADDING DETAIL TO THE FIG LEAVES

Next dab your brush into green and dot around a section of leaf, then blend yellow next to that area of leaf. Repeat this with other greens and lighter blue in random patches on each leaf, blending as you go. The leaf will start to appear three-dimensional.

Step 7

PAINTING THE FIG FRUIT

Repeat this process for the fig fruit. Using light pink and yellow, brush upward in the direction of the stripes on a fig. Then take a darker green and orange on one brush and sweep up again at the edge. Finally, take a darker violet and pink on your brush and sweep next to it.

Step 8

BLENDING EDGES

Using a smaller pointed brush dabbed in dark violet or darker green, carefully go around some edges of a leaf or fig. Use a dry brush (size 16 filbert or round) to blend this dark edge of the leaf or fruit; this creates variation of light to look like a natural edge.

Step 9

ADDING LEAF VEINS

Load a fine size 4 liner brush with a little water and some white paint. Very carefully paint some thin lines to indicate veins down the centre of each fig leaf. Leave gaps in places – you don't need to paint all the lines. Work your way across the wall, leaving out sections of leaf. You can always return; less is more. Look carefully at your images of fig leaves to mimic the direction of the veins. The angle is important to make it realistic.

GRAPHIC BOTANICAL MURAL

This type of mural is painted in the flat graphic style and is made up of interlocking flat shapes in single paint colours. Unlike the Abstract Geometric Mural, there is no need for masking (low-stick) tape because there are no straight edges. This is a striking modern design that nevertheless uses the softness and fluidity of nature. Here we use a palette of nine colours, but you can change the colours to suit your space and interior. You need to get a feel for the leaf shapes before launching onto the wall, so preparation line drawings are vital. Stick to four or five species of plant; in this mural we have chosen a tropical theme.

SKILL LEVEL:

Materials and tools

PREP WORK:

- Roll of lining paper
- Pencil
- Selection of leaf images
- Sketchbook or paper
- Colour sample sheet

PAINTING THE MURAL:

- Dust sheet (drop cloth)
- Stepladder
- 2H or 3H pencil
- Selection of brushes in mixed shapes and sizes: medium-size flat, pointed rounds sizes 6 to 8, blunt rounds
- Two large glass jars of water to clean brushes
- Sample pots of paint in five to nine colours

WE HAVE USED CRAIG & ROSE TROUBADOUR (BRIGHT RED), FLEURIE (BLUE-GREEN), TAPESTRY GREEN (SAGE GREEN), DEEP ADAM GREEN (MEDIUM GREEN), FRENCH TURQUOISE (DARK TURQUOISE) AND TINTERN STONE (CREAM), FARROW & BALL IN BANCHA (DARK OLIVE) AND LITTLE GREENE PAINT IN CANTON (DEEP BLUE-GREEN) AND GREEN VERDITER (BRIGHT BLUE-GREEN) IN THIS MURAL.

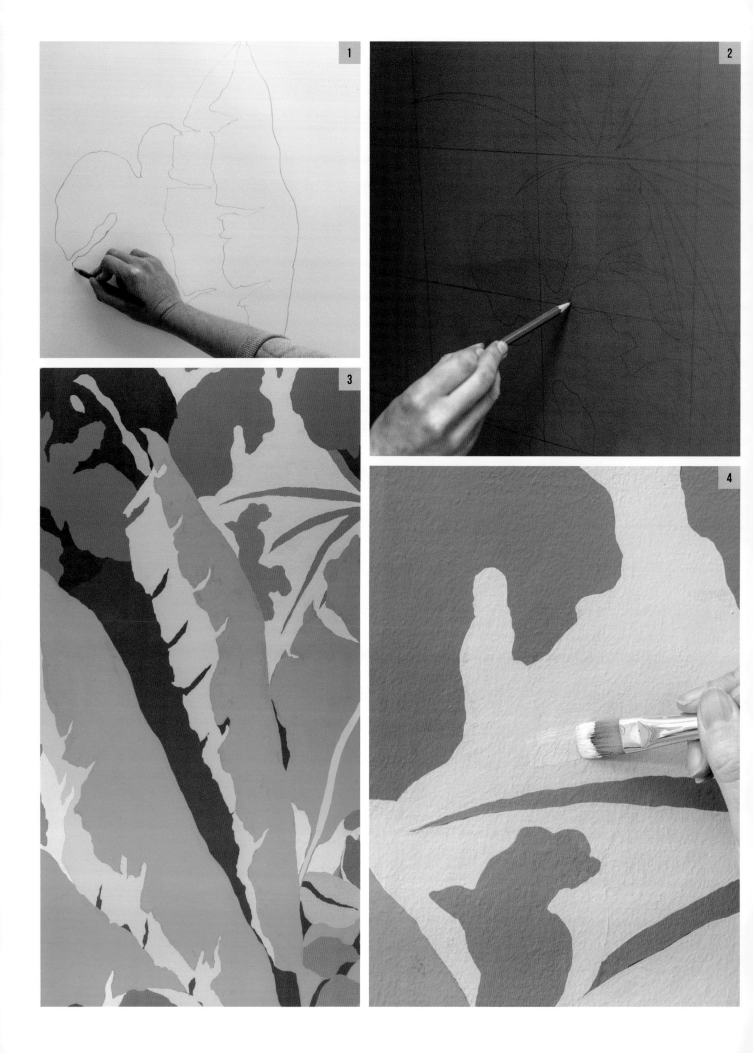

Step 1

PRACTISING THE SHAPES

Experiment with leaf shapes and composition on lining paper, overlapping each shape. Start by drawing an initial flat shape and then draw a different species behind it. Repeat until your paper is covered. This will create moments of negative space in random shapes, which you can paint in using one of your chosen colours. We always draw freehand onto the wall, but you may find it easier to cut out large stencils to draw around using your lining paper.

Step 2

PENCILLING YOUR DESIGN ONTO THE WALL

Either draw or stencil the shape of the leaves onto the wall using a 2H or 3H pencil. Make sure you have a range of leaves, some with softer edges and others with spikes – this will bring a punctuation to your design. Don't worry if you make a mistake, remember every part of the wall will be painted over.

Step 3

PAINTING THE LEAVES

Decide which colour you want to use for each species of leaf. In our design the banana leaves are painted in two different types of green in order to create a vein and the impression of a folded leaf. Use a medium-size flat brush for the larger areas and to paint flatter edges. Start with the paint in the middle of the shapes and brush toward the edge; this will help to keep a smooth finish on the wall. The strength of this design is in the neat edges – use a pointed paintbrush in sizes 6 to 8 for the pointed ends of leaves and spikier plants. Do not load your brush too heavily, you can always add more paint. You don't want the design to become blobby.

Step 4

FILLING IN THE NEGATIVE SPACE

You will find that areas of negative space will be left in interesting shapes between some leaves. Using your chosen colours, fill in these spaces – being careful to keep neat edges. You do not need to limit the negative space to one colour. If you are happy with the background colour your wall is already painted in, you can leave these spaces unpainted.

Step 5

LAYERING UP

You will need to paint two or three further layers in order to get completely flat, brushstroke-free shapes. You can use the paint more sparingly at this stage, blending over the top of the larger shapes with a medium-size flat brush.

CHILDREN'S MURAL

This mural is based on the London Underground map. This simplistic design adds a wonderful pop of colour to a child's room without dominating the space. The abstract quality of the design will give a longevity to the mural because it is not overtly childish in design, so should see your little one through into their teenage years. We have chosen a limited palette, focusing on seven colours, but you could incorporate as many colours as you like. You could even choose another map to base your design on. How about the Paris Metro or New York Subway? This mural is all about straight lines. Measuring is key to keeping the width of the lines correct. Take your time mapping out your design with the masking (low-stick) tape.

SKILL LEVEL:

ACRYLICS CAN FEEL LESS SMOOTH WHEN APPLYING TO WALLS – AND THERE ARE ENVIRONMENTAL CONCERNS ON LARGER AREAS (SEE INFO ON VOCS IN PAINT SECTION). BUT ACRYLICS LEND THEMSELVES WELL TO THIS STYLE OF MURAL IN A CHILD'S ROOM BECAUSE:

A THE DESIGN HAS LOTS OF THIN FLAT LINES. ACRYLIC PAINT HAS A RICH CONSISTENCY AND PROVIDES A SHOT OF INTENSE COLOUR.

B IT'S VERY HARDWEARING ONCE DRY. 'TRADITIONAL' ACRYLIC PAINT IS WATERPROOF SO ANY CHILDREN'S MESS CAN BE WIPED AWAY.

C THERE'S NO WASTAGE AS YOU CAN BUY IT IN SMALL POTS. LEFTOVER PAINT CAN BE GIVEN TO THE CHILDREN TO PAINT WITH!

WE LIKE GOLDEN FLUID ACRYLICS AS THESE ARE HIGH QUALITY.

Materials and tools

PREP WORK:

- Sketchbook
- Coloured pencils
- Underground map reference
- Tracing paper
- Light box (optional)
- Loose paper for light box
- Ruler
- Set square
- Metre (yard) stick ruler
- 2H pencil
- Masking (low-stick) tape
- Credit card for smoothing down tape
- Colour sample sheet

PAINTING THE MURAL:

- Dust sheet (drop cloth)
- Small stepladder (optional)
- Selection of small pointed round and flat brushes in sizes 4 to 12
- Selection of acrylic paints in blue, orange, yellow, red, green, black and pink
- Roll of paper towel and J Cloth
- Several glass jars of water to clean brushes

Step 1

SKETCHING THE DESIGN

Practise sketching out your design on paper with coloured pencils. You could trace over a printout of metro/tube line or copy freehand. If tracing, a light box is very useful – Clara borrows her nine-year-old's lightbox for this purpose! The key thing to remember is that all the angles must correspond to each other. Use a ruler to draw the lines, and to create the right angles we find using a set square useful.

Step 2

PENCILLING YOUR DESIGN ONTO THE WALL

Once you are happy with your design it's time to draw it up onto the wall. It's worth marking off points along the wall with your metre (yard) stick to make sure your horizontal lines are straight. You could choose a method from our scaling up technique (see Preparation: Scaling Up for the possible options), but if possible we do recommend drawing straight onto the wall using your paper and pencil design. It will be more straightforward.

Step 3

TAPING THE LINES

Now it's time to start taping up. Do refer to Technical Painting Styles: Flat Graphic Style for a reminder on how to use masking tape. Again, check your taped lines are straight using the metre stick as you tape.

Step 4

BEGINNING TO PAINT

You are now ready to start applying the paint. Remember to always start from the outside of the tape, moving your brush inward to the middle of your line to avoid the paint bleeding under the tape. Start with the red of the central line, which will wrap around the room. Using a dry small flat brush with a minimal amount of paint, brush over the tape toward the middle of the line. Allow to dry and then add a second layer. Once thoroughly dry very carefully peel off the masking tape.

Step 5

ADDING A SECOND COAT

Repeat the application of the paint for each colour. Make sure you allow sufficient drying time and use the paint sparsely – two coats should be sufficient.

Step 6

PAINTING CURVED LINES

In order to create a curve in the lines where they transition from horizontal to diagonal, we suggest painting freehand with a small pointed round brush.

Step 7

REMOVING THE TAPE

Once you have completed all the lines, have a cup of tea whilst you wait for the paint to dry. Once dry, begin peeling away the tape very carefully – remembering to peel backward in a tight angled pull. This will cause less damage and leaves a clearer line.

Step 8

TOUCHING UP

Once all the tape is removed, use a small paintbrush to touch up any areas that might need correcting.

THIS IS THE ONLY MURAL IN THE BOOK WHERE WE RECOMMEND ACRYLIC PAINT. WE USE EMULSION (ACRYLIC LATEX) FOR MOST PROJECTS BECAUSE IT BLENDS WELL, IS EASY TO APPLY AND LESS EXPENSIVE FOR LARGE AREAS.

BIRDS AND ANIMALS

This theme is a lot of fun and less tricky than you might think. The mural we have chosen has a tropical setting: a graphic banana tree with a monkey climbing up it and two little birds. Of course, you can paint any animal you choose and can add as many creatures as you wish – and paint in any style. We draw our animals freehand, but there are shapes in the Templates section that you can use, or you can find your own imagery and cut it out. Your animals and birds need to be in a setting: unless you are doing a pure animal mural, it looks great to have greenery or trees. For instance, a branch is lovely for an owl or a parrot to be perching upon. Play around in your sketchbook with cuttings and scale first; do you want little birds that flutter through your mural or do you want larger scale for impact?

SKILL LEVEL:

WE HAVE USED LITTLE GREENE PAINTS GREEN VERDITER (BRIGHT BLUE-GREEN), FARROW & BALL NANCY'S BLUSHES (DEEP PINK) AND CORNFORTH WHITE (PALE GREY-WHITE), ALONG WITH CRAIG & ROSE SUNG BLUE (LIGHT BLUE-GREEN), FLEURIE (BLUE-GREEN), LAMPLIGHTER (DARK YELLOW) AND DAMSON (DARK RED-BROWN) IN THIS MURAL.

Materials and tools

PREP WORK:

- Roll of lining paper
- Pencil
- Templates – banana leaf, monkey, birds
- Sketchbook or paper
- Colour sample sheet

PAINTING THE MURAL:

- Dust sheet (drop cloth)
- Stepladder
- Selection of brushes for the banana tree sizes 10 to 16 in mixed shapes: pointed rounds, blunt rounds, flat and filbert
- Selection of very fine brushes for the creatures sizes 2 to 10: in particular good number of filbert and pointed rounds
- Jars filled with water for cleaning brushes
- Roll of paper towel and a J Cloth
- Sample pots of paint: several different greens, blues, oranges, reds, pinks, yellows, brown, gold
- Masking (low-stick) tape
- 2H pencil

Step 1

DRAWING THE BANANA TREE

For this stage you could follow the steps in the Graphic Botanical Mural or the Painterly Botanical Mural but draw just one banana tree. Decide on a shape you like – perhaps big fat leaves or more broken wind-blown shapes – and practise drawing them out. When you have decided on a design, choose your scaling up technique (see Preparation: Scaling Up for the various options) and draw your banana tree onto the wall. We have chosen to ground our tree and have the branches fanning outwards – this allows branches for the birds to occupy. The tall trunk is for the monkey.

Step 2

GRAPHIC BOTANICAL BANANA LEAVES

Decide which style you want to use to paint your leaves. For the graphic botanical style, as shown here, choose a lovely soft green for the leaves, with some leaves in a deeper green and maybe a pale blue-green leaf in the background. Or you could go yellow or even pink!

Step 3

PAINTERLY BOTANICAL BANANA LEAVES

For the painterly botanical style, great colours for the leaves would be dark yellow and greens with a pale blue-green sweeping through.

Step 4

GRAPHIC BOTANICAL STEM

Painting the leaves first means that stems can be painted in around them to look more natural. Make sure to paint a branch that comes through the leaves, ready for a bird to perch upon. Whichever style you chose for the leaves, stick with the same for the stem. If you chose the graphic botanical style you could match the same colour to your leaves, or you might choose to paint the stems in another colour.

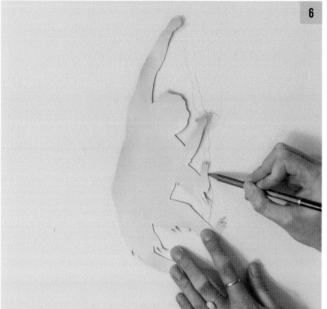

Step 5

PAINTERLY BOTANICAL STEM

If you are doing the painterly botanical leaf style, then go for it with colours. Don't go too dark – stick with paler hues of gold, green and yellows for the stem.

Step 6

DRAWING THE MONKEY

Using the monkey from the Templates section or your own images, hold the monkey up to the trunk. You want it to appear to be scampering up the stem, so feet and hands should be positioned on the stem. Draw around it. Don't worry about wobbly lines – you will paint this in afterwards.

Step 7

DRAWING THE BIRDS

Copy one of the bird from the Templates section, cut out and then hold up to one of the branches you drew in earlier that forks between the leaves. Draw around the bird carefully. The feet do not need to show, but can if you wish. Cut out the flying bird in the same way and position it wherever you like – we normally have it fluttering inward toward to the tree. Draw around it in pencil.

Step 8

DRAWING IN THE DETAIL

This part is where you need your eye because you will be copying exactly from the template as much as possible. Use masking tape to stick the template of each bird and monkey next to your drawn outlines on the wall. Use a hard pencil sharpened well (2H) to carefully draw in the shapes of the wings and any variations in feather sections, eyes and so on.

Step 9
PAINTING THE BIRD'S DETAILED FEATHERS

Choose a pink, pale grey-white, blue, yellow, pink and white. Take a medium pointed round brush size 4 and delicately fill each section of the bird with a subtle base colour in pink or grey-white. Dip a size 2 or 3 pointed round brush into the blues and, beginning at the side wing dab little marks to indicate feathers. Dip again into yellow and add yellow, then pink. Cover all sections of the bird – you will need to change up a brush size for larger areas of feather. Follow the direction of feathers in your template image to be most realistic.

Step 10
ADDING HIGHLIGHTS AND DEPTH

It's important to allow white dabs to come last. These can be sporadic and help bring depth. Start with the lightest at the highest point at the breast and change the tone as you work to the edges of the bird to indicate a three-dimensional body. Avoid painting the eye area – just leave the shape unpainted for now. Once your bird is dry, use a very fine liner or pointed round brush size 3 to dab dark red-brown all over the feathers to create depth and three dimensionality.

Step 11
PAINTING THE MONKEY

Take a medium pointed round brush size 4 and delicately fill each section of the monkey with pale grey-white. Dab a size 4 or 6 pointed round brush with brown and white and paint the shapes of colour in as precisely as possible, copying the monkey template. Work downward – darker for the head, lighter for the outside of the body, darker at the middle. Work in the same way as for the bird, only this time with longer sweeps and less brushy as you are not creating feathers. Leave the eye area unpainted.

Step 12
PAINTING THE EYES AND FINISHING THE MONKEY

Use a small round brush size 2 to fill each eye completely with black. When the eye is dry, return with pure white on a clean brush. Dot two tiny white dots in the centre of each eye. Use the white to dab in extra light streaks onto the tail or hands of the monkey as a finishing touch.

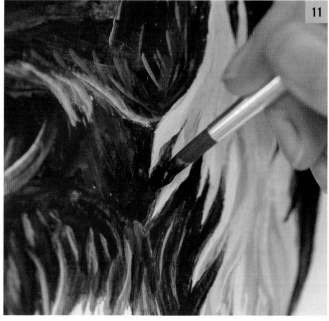

LINEAR MURAL

This is in effect a line drawing on a wall and there is very little painting required. You could use a fine brush with emulsion (acrylic latex) for a more painterly line, but we use Posca pens, which are easy and quick – though they do require a little getting used to. A linear mural can be a sleek 'less is more' minimal statement, or a buzz of exciting lines covering every inch of your wall. The sky is the limit in terms of subject matter – your design could be representational or abstract or something in between. There are also methods of advancing the technique if you wish, in Step 7. The linear technique works well on top of a strong base colour, such as dark blue or green – a gold line over the top would bring glamour. Or hot pink neon over a pale orange base would look amazing.

SKILL LEVEL:

WE HAVE USED FARROW & BALL DOWNPIPE (ALMOST BLACK)
FOR THE BACKGROUND OF OUR MURAL.

Materials and tools

PREP WORK:

- Dust sheet (drop cloth)
- Stepladder
- Two small rollers and tray (if painting the base coat yourself)
- Almost black emulsion (acrylic latex)
- Sketchbook or paper
- Pencil
- Templates – banana leaf, bird of paradise plant, agave plant, monstera leaf, tropical fern, fatsia leaf (or other plants of your choice)
- Colour sample sheet
- Ruler
- 2H pencil
- Masking (low-stick) tape

PAINTING THE MURAL:

- White Posca pens in sizes PC-3M, PC-5M, PC-7M
- Large sheet of thick card or paper (for dabbing your Posca pens)
- Couple of thin filbert or fine round brushes
- Glass jar of water to clean brushes
- Roll of paper towel and two J Cloths
- Sample pots of paint in: white, deep pink, orange, yellow, green

Step 1

PREPARING THE WALL

Begin by painting the entire mural area in an almost black shade – see Preparing the Wall: Preparing Interior Walls and follow the steps for preparation and base coat coverage. You will need to use a roller and will need to paint two coats for a deeper hue.

Step 2

DRAWING OUT THE DESIGN

Have a go drawing the plants out freestyle in your sketchbook. You might surprise yourself. Alternatively, you could also use the tropical linear shapes from the Templates section. Copy and cut out the template and lay on the sketchbook, then draw the shapes, copying the image from right to left. We recommend the grid method to scale up (see Preparation: Scaling Up) – the doodle method will not work here because you will not be painting over the doodles.

Step 3

FREESTYLE DRAWING

Using your pencil, draw the design onto the wall beginning at the left. Draw in the banana leaves from the ground upward, then move along to draw the bird of paradise plant in the centre. Lastly, on far left, draw in the agave. Begin drawing each plant at the base as if you are 'growing' the plant – this will help your plants appear more natural.

Step 4

TEMPLATE DRAWING

If you don't want to draw freehand, you can use the plants in the Templates section. Copy and cut out the shapes, then stick them to the wall with masking tape. Draw around the banana leaf, bird of paradise and agave plants with pencil, trying to overlap the shapes at the leaf tips to be more natural. For the monstera and the ferns layer the templates over the top and draw around them. Make sure you stop the lines where larger foliage shapes have already been drawn.

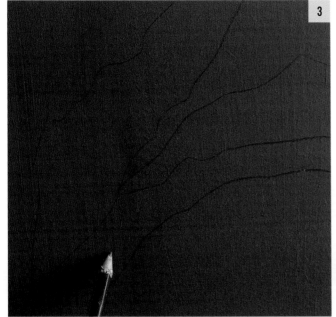

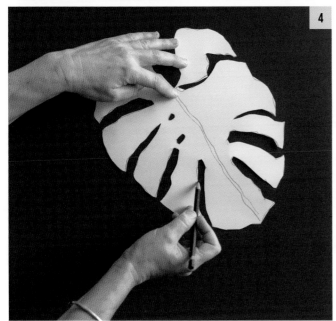

TRY TO KEEP YOUR DRAWING VERY LOOSE AND FLUID, AND LET THE SHAPES MEANDER OVER THE WALL. IF YOU THINK YOU MIGHT HAVE MADE A MISTAKE, DON'T WORRY! THE DENSENESS OF THE DESIGN WILL SOON ABSORB ANYTHING THAT LOOKS A LITTLE OUT OF PLACE.

Step 5

PREPARING THE POSCA PENS

Now it's time to draw over your pencil lines with Posca. You can either use a finer PC-3M or the fatter PC-5M – it's your choice, so experiment over your drawn image in your sketchbook. After opening each pen, make sure to shake it up and down rigorously to dispel the paint into the tip. You then need to press the tip up and down on your sheet of paper to get the flow going.

Step 6

FINALIZING THE LINES

We begin with the PC-3M. Begin tracing over the lines of the first three elements – the banana, bird of paradise and agave, working from the left side to the right side of the wall. In places you can break it up and use a fat tip Posca such as a PC-7M to add some thicker lines. Take care to stick to the line so pencil doesn't peek out.

Step 7

ADDING DEFINITION

Once you have drawn everything all up, you may well need to go around again. Take care to go over the existing line slowly, to keep the line crisp and neat with no paler sections. You will certainly need to do two layers if you have chosen white lines over a dark background.

Step 8

OPTIONAL EXTRA: ADDING PAINTED FLOWERS

You can leave the mural as it is, or you could add some flowers between random leaves. Draw the outline of each flower using one of the shapes from the Templates section. Underpaint the flower shape with white paint as a base over the dark background, so that the top colour will sing. Use pink paint to colour in some of the buds and the petals. Then, with a fresh brush, fill in some orange and yellow petals. Lastly, colour the base of the flower with a little touch of green where the leaves might sit.

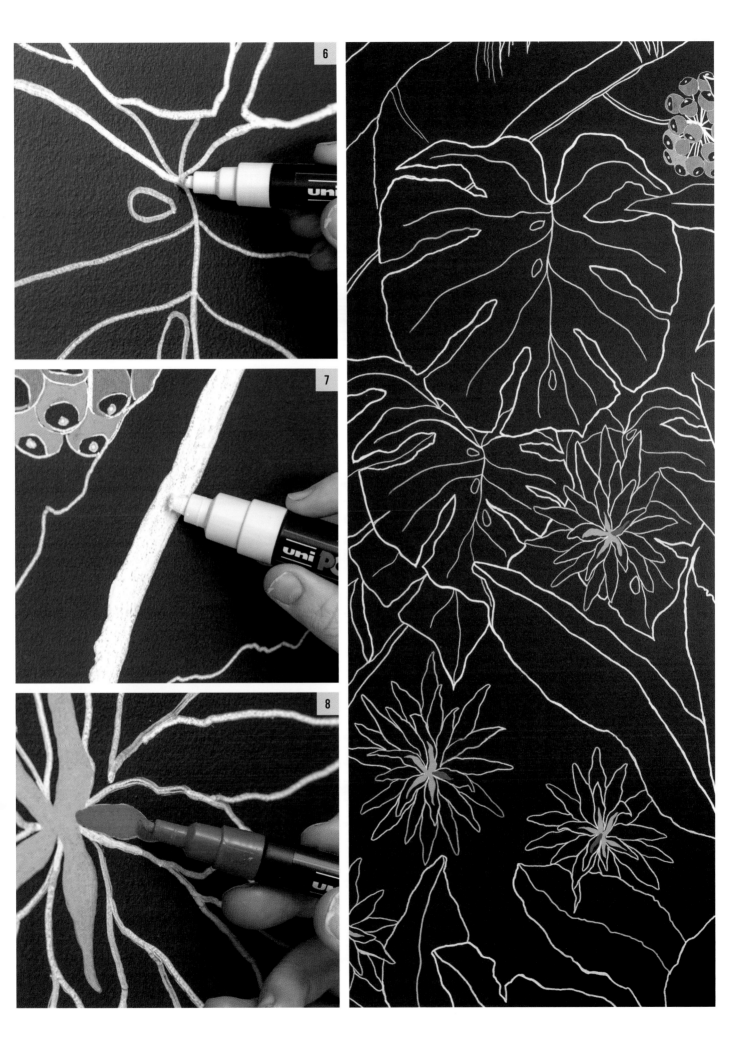

TEMPLATES

Each of these templates can be photocopied and enlarged to the size you need them to best fit your wall. You can also download printable versions of the templates from www.davidandcharles.com.

THE EXTRA INTERNAL LINES ON THE TEMPLATES ARE THERE FOR GUIDANCE WHEN COLOURING AND ADDING DETAILS.

DARK BACKGROUND MURAL

Geranium Flowers

Geranium Leaves

Camellia Leaves

DARK BACKGROUND MURAL

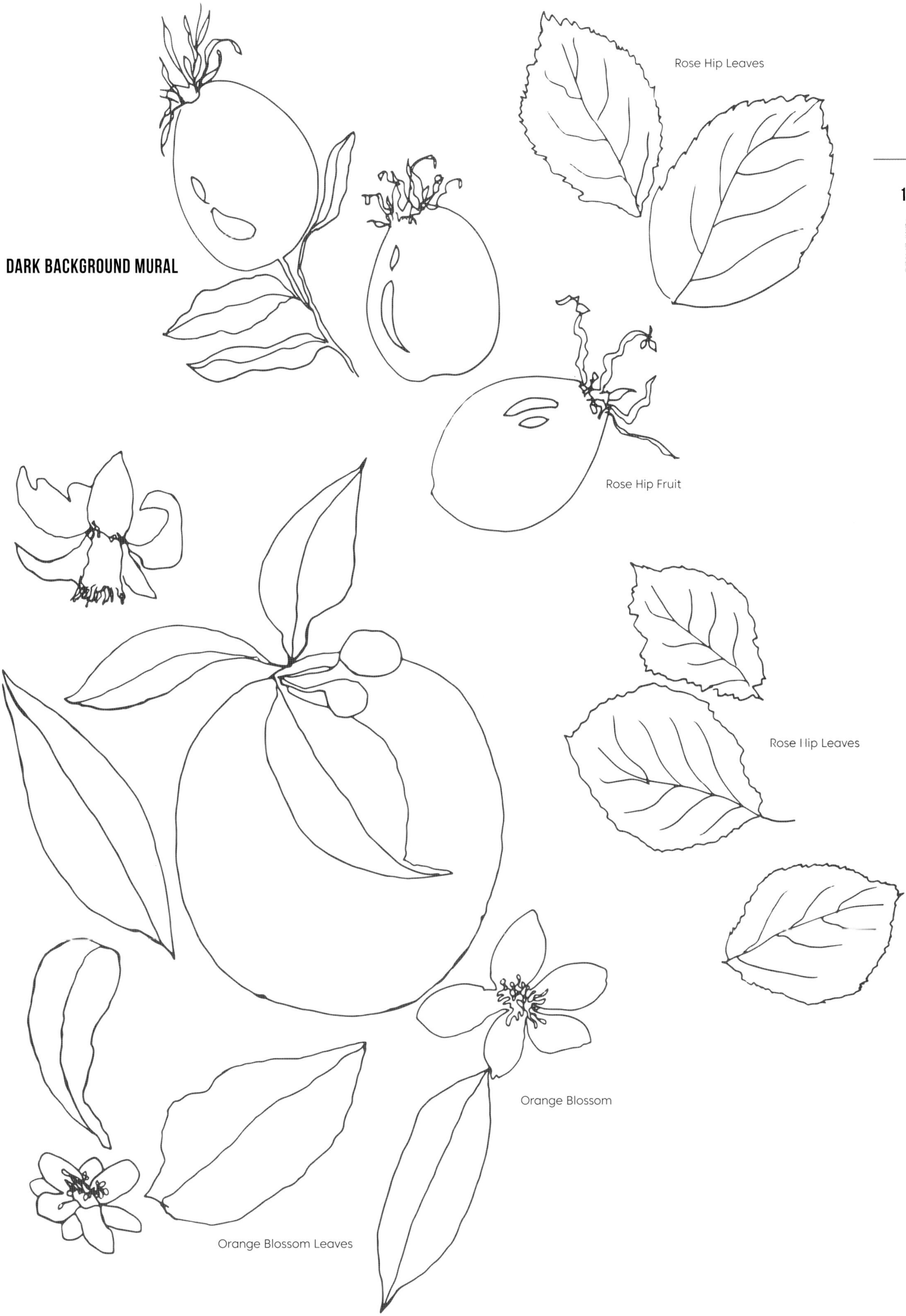

Rose Hip Leaves

Rose Hip Fruit

Rose Hip Leaves

Orange Blossom

Orange Blossom Leaves

MESSY BRUSH STROKES MURAL

Lotus Flower

Rose

**EXTERIOR WALL AND
PAINTERLY BOTANICAL MURAL**

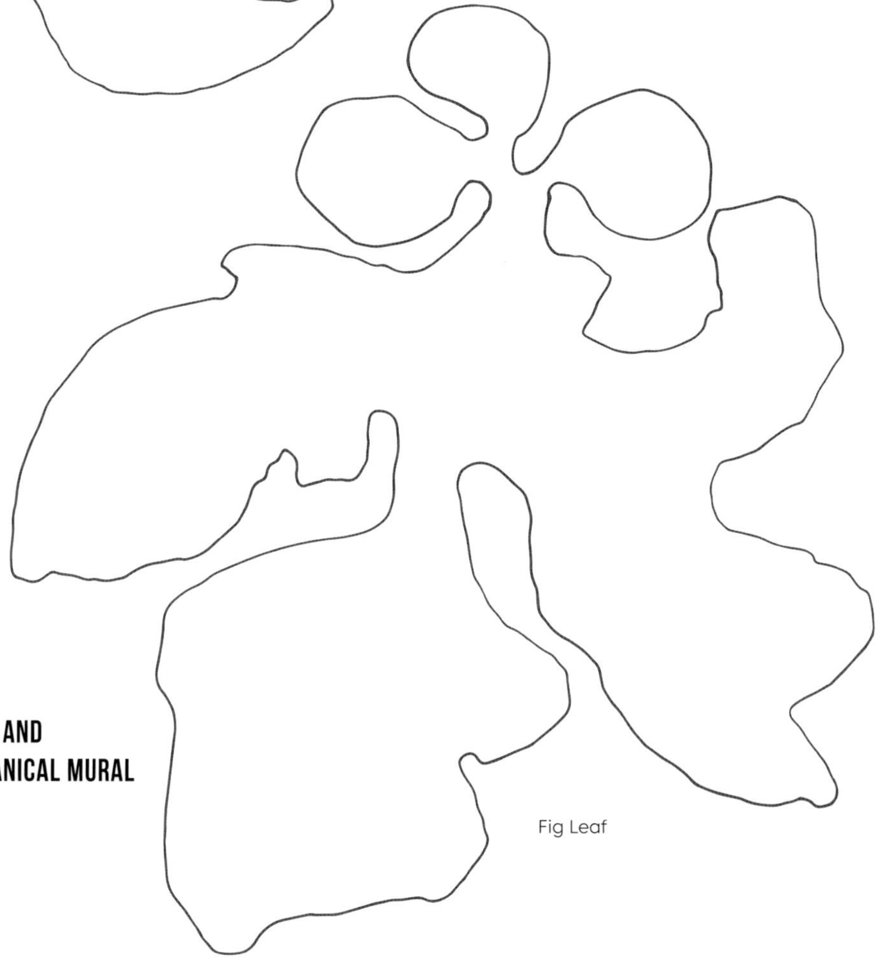

Fig Leaf

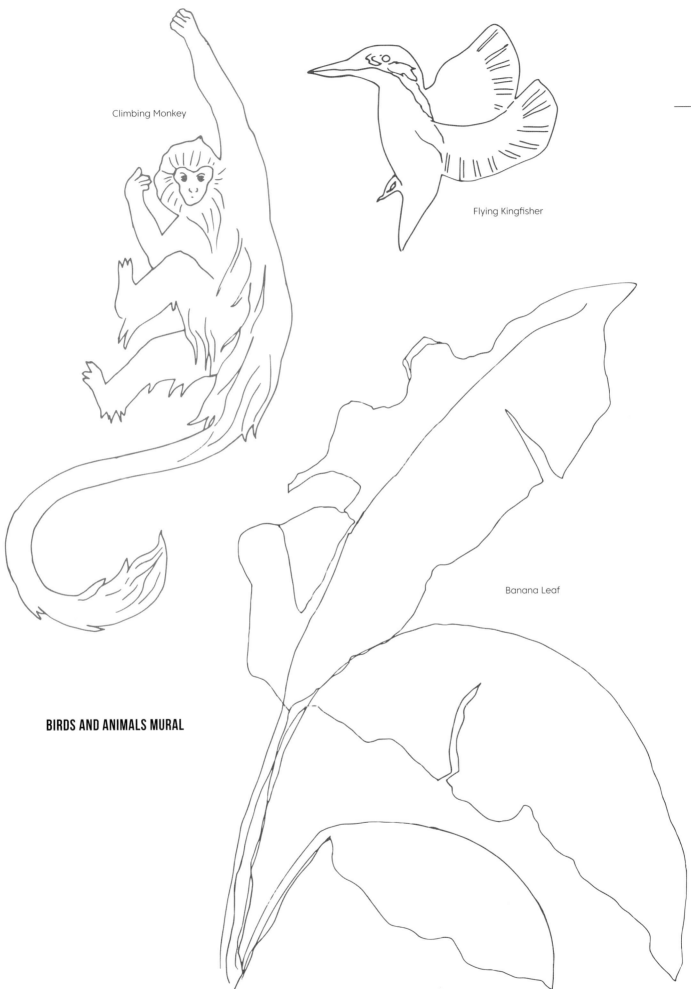

Climbing Monkey

Flying Kingfisher

Banana Leaf

BIRDS AND ANIMALS MURAL

**BIRDS AND
ANIMALS MURAL**

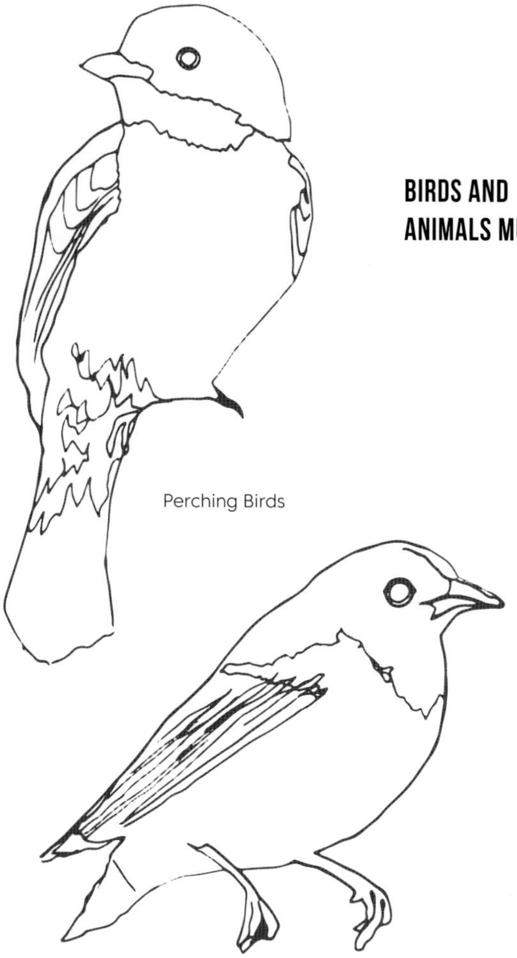

Perching Birds

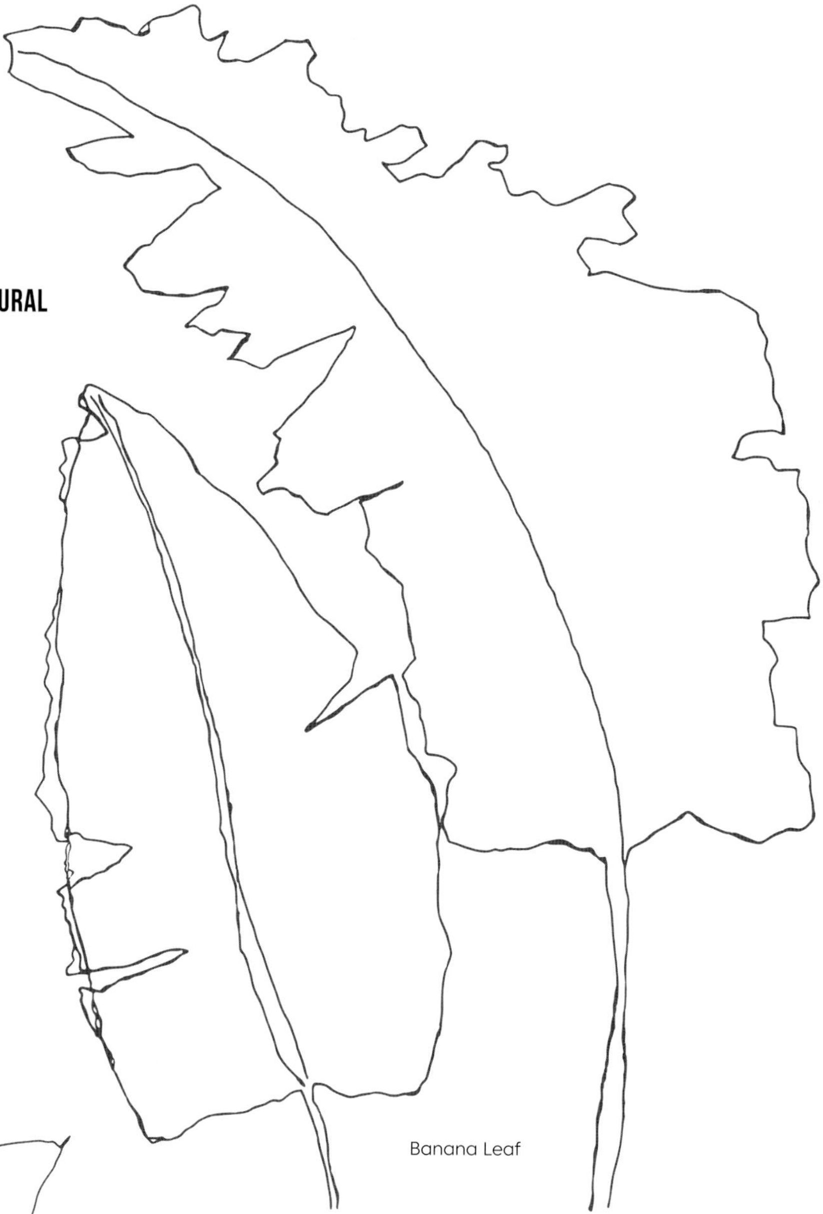

Banana Leaf

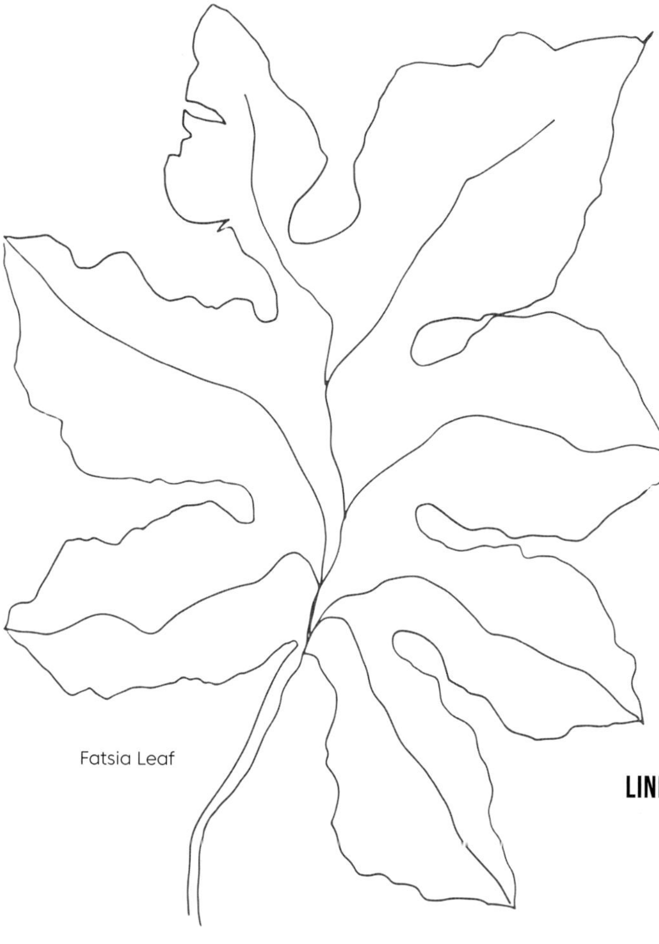

Fatsia Leaf

LINEAR MURAL

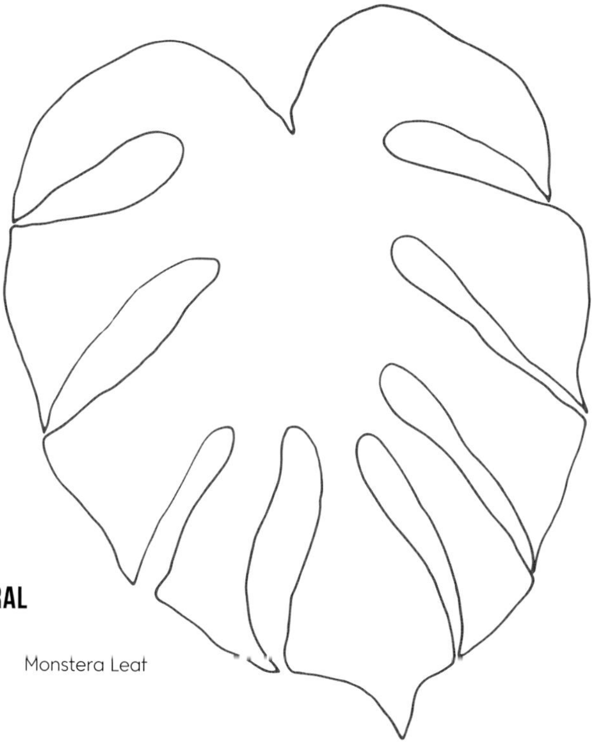

Monstera Leaf

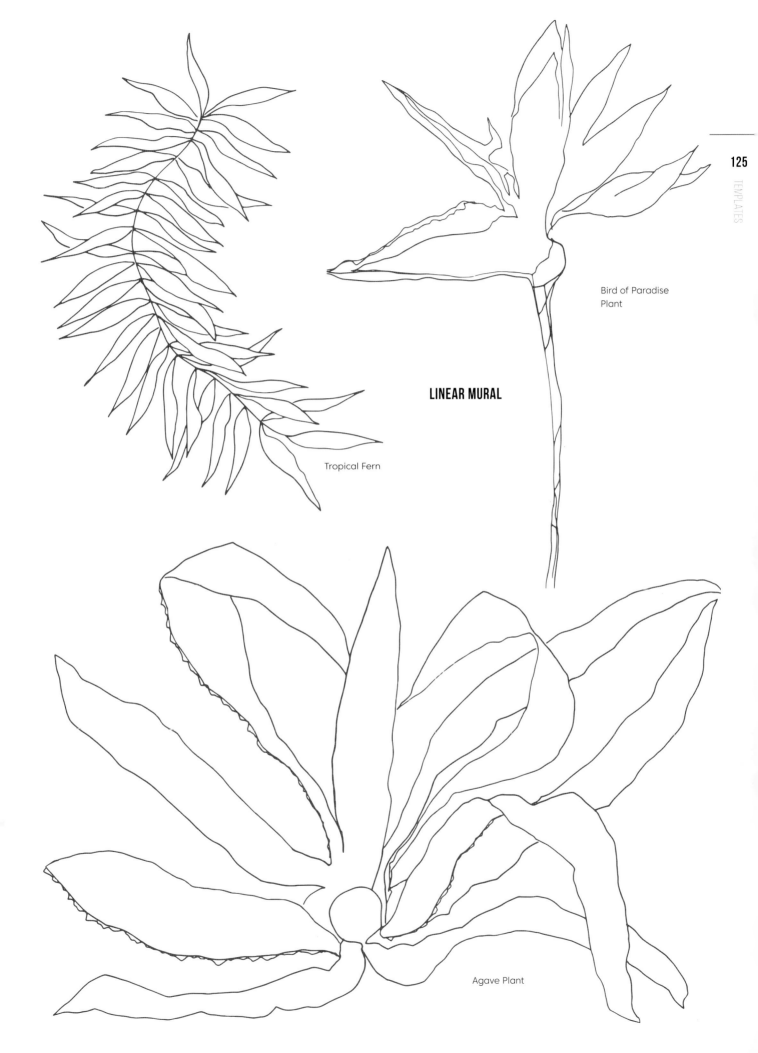

Bird of Paradise
Plant

LINEAR MURAL

Tropical Fern

Agave Plant

SUPPLIERS

Pro Arte brushes
https://www.proarte.co.uk

Da Vinci brushes
https://www.davinci-defet.com

Brewer's Albany decorators' (mottler) brushes
https://www.brewers.co.uk/products/brushes/paint-brushes

Staedtler drawing pens
https://www.staedtler.com/uk/en/

Winsor & Newton sketchpads and large sheets
https://www.winsornewton.com/uk/

Posca pens
https://www.posca.com/en-uk/

Craig & Rose paint
https://www.craigandrose.com

Farrow & Ball paint
https://www.farrow-ball.com

Little Greene paint
https://www.littlegreene.com

Earthborn paint
https://earthbornpaints.co.uk

Lakeland Paints
https://www.lakelandpaints.co.uk

Paint & Paper Library paints
https://www.paintandpaperlibrary.com

Edward Bulmer paints
https://www.edwardbulmerpaint.co.uk

Victory Colours
https://www.victorycolours.co.uk

Golden Fluid Acrylics
https://www.goldenpaints.com

Sandtex Stabilising Solution
https://www.sandtexpaints.com

Polyvine Decorators Varnish
https://www.polyvine.com

Eco Friendly Stone and Brick Cleaner from World of Clean
https://www.worldofclean.co.uk

Daler-Rowney sketchbooks
https://www.daler-rowney.com

Derwent pencils
https://www.derwentart.com

Faber-Castell pencils
https://www.faber-castell.com

SUITABLE STENCILS

Cass Art
https://www.cassart.co.uk

Jackson's
https://www.jacksonsart.com

B&Q
https://www.diy.com

Brewers
https://www.brewers.co.uk

Homebase
https://www.homebase.co.uk

CLOTHING SUPPLIERS

White painting dungarees:
Portwest
https://portwest.com/market/

Navy blue French boiler suits:
VETRA made in France
https://www.vetra.fr/en/

ABOUT THE AUTHORS

Living Wall Murals was established by Clara Wilkinson and Mary West in 2017.

Working as freelance artists, having studied fine art – Clara at Central St. Martins and Mary at the Slade – we wanted to pool our forty years of combined experience. We love nature and share a similar aesthetic for art, design and interiors, so our collaboration was born.

We began by experimenting in colour and scale and, through word of mouth, our mural business grew. We now specialize in finely painted murals for commercial and domestic spaces. Our style ranges from the bold and graphic, to delicate detailed foliage – and we also sell giclée prints of our work. When we are not painting murals, we work as independent artists in our own studios – Clara in Brighton and Mary in London – making, exhibiting and selling our artwork.

ACKNOWLEDGEMENTS

Thank you to our sons and our immediate families.

Thanks to the team at David & Charles.

Thanking Jason and Sarah Rowntree for their help; we were lucky enough to work with them closely.

Thank you to our clients, who have been so helpful allowing us to revisit projects and shoot.

INDEX

Credits

The photographs in this book were taken by Jason Jenkins, apart from:

P.23 (tl) Juan Rojas (Unsplash)

P.25 (m and bl) Jimmy Palmer

P.33 (bl) and P.65 (tr) Clara Wilkinson

P.49 (tl) Jesse Bowser (Unsplash),
(bl) Pawel Czerwinski (Unsplash), (br) Benjamin Faust (Unsplash)

P.87 (bl) Theme Photos (Unsplash)

Thank you to everyone who allowed their murals to be featured in this book:

- Highgate House (London)
- Kusaki Restaurant (Brighton)
- Pai Skincare (London)
- Romeo and Juliet Cafe (London)
- Whisper (Kew)
- Ben and Maria Mays
- Claudia McVie
- James and Vanessa Townsend

A DAVID AND CHARLES BOOK
© David and Charles, Ltd 2022

David and Charles is an imprint of David and Charles, Ltd
Suite A, Tourism House, Pynes Hill, Exeter, EX2 5WS

Text and Designs © Clara Wilkinson and Mary West 2022
Layout and Photography © David and Charles, Ltd 2022

First published in the UK and USA in 2022

A catalogue record for this book is available from the British Library.

ISBN-13: 9781446309360 paperback
ISBN-13: 9781446381823 EPUB
ISBN-13: 9781446381816 PDF

This book has been printed on paper from approved suppliers and made from pulp from sustainable sources.

Printed in UK by Short Run Press for:
David and Charles, Ltd
Suite A, Tourism House, Pynes Hill, Exeter, EX2 5WS

10 9 8 7 6 5 4 3 2 1

Publishing Director: Ame Verso
Senior Commissioning Editor: Sarah Callard
Managing Editor: Jeni Chown
Editor: Jessica Cropper
Project Editor: Marie Clayton
Head of Design: Anna Wade
Designers: Lucy Waldron and Sarah Rowntree
Pre-press Designer: Ali Stark
Art Direction: Sarah Rowntree
Photography: Jason Jenkins
Production Manager: Beverley Richardson

David and Charles publishes high-quality books on a wide range of subjects. For more information visit www.davidandcharles.com.

Share your makes with us on social media using #dandcbooks and follow us on Facebook and Instagram by searching for @dandcbooks.

Layout of the digital edition of this book may vary depending on reader hardware and display settings.